THE FORBIDDEN DAUGHTER

The Forbidden Daughter

The True Story of a Holocaust Survivor

ZIPORA KLEIN JAKOB

HARPER

NEW YORK • LONDON • TORONTO • SYDNEY

HARPER

HarperCollins books may be purchased for educational, business, or sales promotional use. For information, please email the Special Markets Department at SPsales@harpercollins.com.

Originally published as *Elida, the Forbidden Ghetto Girl* in 2021 by Adam & Eve Agencies (1995) LTD.

FIRST HARPER PAPERBACKS EDITION PUBLISHED 2024.

Designed by Jamie Lynn Kerner

Library of Congress Cataloging-in-Publication Data

Names: Klein Jakob, Zipora, author.
Title: The forbidden daughter : a biographical novel of the Holocaust / Zipora Klein Jakob.
Description: First edition. | New York, NY : Harper Paperbacks, 2024.
Identifiers: LCCN 2023034822 | ISBN 9780063296657 (trade paperback) | ISBN 9780063296664 (ebook)
Subjects: LCSH: Katzman, Elida. | Holocaust, Jewish (1939-1945)--Lithuania--Kaunas--Fiction. | Jewish children in the Holocaust--Fiction. | LCGFT: Biographical fiction. | Historical fiction. | Novels.
Classification: LCC PR9510.9.K386 F67 2024 | DDC 823/.92--dc23/eng/20231204
LC record available at https://lccn.loc.gov/2023034822

ISBN 978-0-06-329665-7 (pbk.)

24 25 26 27 28 LBC 5 4 3 2 1

In memory of Elida Katzman (Freidman, Goldberg)

In memory of Richard (Dick) Katzman

In memory of Dr. Jonah and Tzila Freidman, who perished in the Kovno Ghetto

A memorial candle for my family members, who perished in the Holocaust

To my uncle Eliezer Goldberg and his wife, Toibeh, who survived the Holocaust and died in their old age as proud and free Jews

Contents

THE FORBIDDEN DAUGHTER

Prologue

WHAT A TURBULENT LIFE AWAITED THAT baby born in the Kovno ghetto! Her name was Elida, which in Hebrew means "nonbirth." Her parents, Dr. Jonah and Tzila Freidman, chose that name in defiance of the ban on childbirth that the Nazis imposed on Jews in Lithuanian ghettos. In this sense, she was a "forbidden" child.

I was twelve when I first met Elida. She came to our family in Haifa from Vilna (Vilnius) in the late 1950s. She was a willowy girl, her eyes dark and sad, with an eagle-like nose, prominent chin, and wavy black hair. She wore plaid dresses that covered her arms and knees. Elida said little, and when she spoke, she spoke Yiddish.

I don't remember how she was introduced to me, what she said, or what the other children of the family told me about her. We did not yet know about the horrors of the Holocaust. Whatever we knew we garnered from the whispers of adults. These pieces of information did not add up to a full story. She came to us from Vilna with an elderly couple, and I understood they were her parents.

But it wasn't clear to me why she was living with one of my aunts and not with her parents.

Several months after her arrival in Haifa, there was a mysterious commotion. The adults often whispered to each other in Yiddish. The subject of their conversation was Elida, but none of them told us, the children, anything about what was happening. Contributing to the unsettled atmosphere was the fact that my uncle Lazar, my mother's brother, came from America, followed by his wife, Toibeh. They often spent time with Elida and pampered her with plenty of presents. A few months later, I was informed that Elida was going with them to America.

A few days after she left, I saw a newspaper spread out on the table at our house. Perhaps my parents purposely left it there for me to read. The headline was THE STORY OF A STRANGE ALLIANCE BETWEEN TWO JEWS IN THE KOVNO GHETTO. The article was about a pact made between my uncle, Lazar Goldberg, and his cousin, Dr. Jonah Freidman, who swore to adopt each other's child if only one of them survived the war.

This article sowed the seed of Elida's story in me. I was obsessed with her name: Elida, the "forbidden" child. I clung to every bit of information I gathered about her and my uncles, and about the Holocaust. I chose to study history at the university because I wanted to understand what had happened.

Many years after the war, Elida and I met again and developed a strong and loving relationship. We first reconnected in June 1973 when she came to Israel as an immigrant, a married woman, and a mother of three children. I couldn't know how her story would end.

About ten years ago, I set out on a journey of thousands of miles to Lithuania and the United States. Conducting dozens of meetings and interviews, I became immersed in the memories and pain of my family members. I tracked down documents, certificates, court records, drawings, and letters in Elida's handwriting. I read books about the periods and events of her life. I incorporated the information that I gathered into the plot of this book and shaped Elida's character as I understood it. I chose to tell the story of her life as a biographical novel.

I understand that some of my family members experienced the events differently. I apologize if I have hurt their feelings by telling the story in a way that diverges from their memories and understanding of the story. In this book, I tell the story of Elida, my cousin, as I experienced and internalized it over the years. I hope the book will immortalize her in the hearts of its readers.

1

The Kovno Ghetto

At the hospital in the Kovno ghetto in 1943, a surgeon named Dr. Jonah Freidman was in a crowded room at a meeting of other doctors. Suddenly, he was summoned to step out and treat a young man who had been shot. The group he left behind were discussing the recent news about the five thousand Jews who were supposed to arrive in Kovno (Kaunas) from Vilna but were murdered in Ponary. Everyone knew this was the beginning of even worse times for the Jews of the Kovno ghetto.

Jonah walked slowly toward the room where the young man was waiting for him. He was very tired. Hardly a day went by without bad news.

"I'm exhausted, we're all exhausted," he muttered to himself. "Every day there's a new decree. Isn't it enough that we have no medicine, that the hospital is packed full, that we find ourselves with fewer doctors and nurses by the day? Now the Nazis want to place German inspectors in the hospital!"

He was perspiring. He ran his fingers through his hair, remembering how just that morning, his wife, Tzila, had pointed out the gray that was spreading across his head. He leaned against the wall. "I must relax," he told himself. He paused, took a deep breath, and hurried toward the room where the wounded man was lying. With his head bowed, he passed the makeshift hospital rooms trying not to hear the moans and cries around him.

Suddenly he heard Tzila calling to him.

"What happened?" he asked in alarm. Although Tzila worked as an assistant in a laboratory near the hospital, they did not usually meet at work, but only in the evenings in the hut they shared with their family in the ghetto.

"Jonah, I have to talk to you, you have to come outside with me."

She had clearly been crying.

"What happened? Who was taken? Who was killed? Are you okay?" He reached out to caress her head in an attempt to calm her down.

"I have to talk to you."

"But I have to go into the operating room!"

"No," she said, "talk to me first. I have something important to tell you, it can't wait."

"What's happened?" he asked, grabbing her shoulders. She pulled him by the arm into the corner.

"I'm pregnant," she whispered.

The sharp contraction in his chest returned. "Are you sure?"

"Yes," she replied. "I haven't had my period for three months."

"That doesn't mean anything. This has happened before. You are not in the best physical condition, you know."

She had known this would be his reaction. She had prepared herself for it.

"This time it's a pregnancy. We have a baby here," she said, pointing to her belly. "I know, and besides, I feel it." She whispered hesitantly, "You should know I visited Dr. Gurevitch. She examined me. I'm pregnant! You know how much I have been waiting for this!" Suddenly, she became even more agitated. "You will not persuade me to give it up! I have been waiting for a baby for four years. I know what you think, but I have desires of my own. I have decided! I will give birth! You must understand that this is my hope!"

"Don't tell anyone," Jonah implored. "We need to plan our next steps. Please don't tell anyone, not even the family."

"Oh, Jonah"—Tzila clenched her fists—"do you always have to be so practical? Even now, instead of hugging me after what I've just told you, you're giving me orders?" She retreated from him, despondent.

Jonah turned with trembling legs toward the room on the second floor where the injured young man was waiting. The news of Tzila's pregnancy had paralyzed him. For several months now, his fellow doctors had been dealing with the law against Jewish women bearing children. Every day he heard about the dilemma of abortion and saw how difficult it was for mothers to make that decision. And he also saw how difficult it was for the doctors who put their lives at risk by helping mothers give birth.

At the latest doctors' meeting, Dr. Elchanan Elkes, a leading physician and head of the Jewish council (*Altesternat*) in the ghetto, reiterated the announcement published in the ghetto that "according to the orders of the governing authorities, the birth of babies in the ghetto is forbidden under penalty of death. All pregnancies must be terminated." Dr. Aharon Peretz was thus busy day and night terminating pregnancies under difficult conditions, endangering the mothers and their families as well as his own family. He was also known for his kindness and sympathy for women who refused to abort.

During the surgery to remove the bullet from the patient's waist, Jonah performed mechanically. He did not put the patient to sleep. "We need to save on anesthetics. You're a young man and you can bear the pain."

This was not like Jonah, who was usually a calm and kind presence for his patients, especially those groaning in agony. Standing beside him, Hanke, his regular nurse, felt that something was wrong with him, that he was not his usual self.

Indeed, thoughts raced through his mind while performing the operation: What kind of world will I be bringing my child into? What chance does he have? What hope? Still, Jonah knew his wife—and he knew he could not rob her of her reason to live. Throughout the day, these thoughts flooded him. If Tzila did give birth, could they keep the baby or would they need to give the child up? Could he prevent Tzila from giving birth and having her own child in all this madness?

When he returned to the hut in the evening, Tzila quickly wrapped herself in a woolen blanket and went out with Jonah to the corner of the yard, where the remains of the vegetable plants were growing. They retreated to that corner whenever they wanted to talk to each other away from the attentive ears of their family. Darkness prevailed. Only a few lights and candles flickered in the windows of the ghetto huts, where the few wooden dwellings were huddled together. Jonah placed a heavy hand on Tzila's shoulders, stroked her hair, sat down in front of her, and then wrapped her hands in his.

"We have to make a wise decision, Tzila. I know how much you've looked forward to having a child, but we must carefully consider the wisdom of bringing a child into this world. Every day we lose children, brothers, sisters, neighbors. How can we talk about creating a new life in such a world? What chance would we be giving our child?"

Tzila straightened up. "God has sent us a sign and a signal. We will create a life. I feel that only the prospect of giving birth, of bringing a child into this world, will keep me alive. I want to believe that the nightmare we live in will end. The prospect of having a child sustains me. When it all ends, what will we say? That we gave up? We surrendered? I can't go out into the woods to fight them, but I can give birth despite their monstrous decree. I want to fight, and this is my way!"

These last words overwhelmed him. He had not thought about it that way, he admitted to himself. After all, maybe this was the way to rebel that he had been seeking all along. Maybe this would be their way of saying no to the Nazis.

Jonah stroked Tzila's head and kissed her. "I love you and will go along with you all the way. We have to make some arrangements so that no one notices."

The next few days were full of action. Jonah explained to the family members who shared the hut with him—including his sister, her husband, and one of his uncles—that they'd have to hurry up and excavate the dugout shelter under the hut because rumors had reached the hospital about a wave of expected "actions." They dug the opening from inside the hut and made sure to scatter the accumulated dirt among the weeds and shrubs in the yard. This work was done only after dark. Tzila stopped working at the hospital. She frequently lay down, saying that she was not feeling well. Her sister-in-law and the other occupants of the hut were annoyed. They whispered, sometimes loud enough for her to hear: "Pampered woman," "Look how she lies there," "Princess!" They were angry that she did not share in the hard work. Jonah defended her: "She is ill, she should be cared for."

IN 1943, THE GHETTO TURNED INTO A CONCENTRATION camp, with Jews killed on sight or sent off on transports. Those who remained were stripped of their last remnants of autonomy. Nonetheless, work at the hospital continued, thanks to the sheer will and morality of the doctors and staff. Medical equipment and medicine were scarce, and the number of doctors also declined. Some of them joined the partisans or found hiding places across the river.

In his distress, Jonah sought the closeness of Aharon, his friend and medical colleague, to relieve his anxieties. Jonah's heart went out to the women who came to consult with Aharon about having an abortion. These were beautiful women who, in what seemed to him like ages ago, had sauntered around in high heels, dressed in the height of fashion. Now they were in hiding.

An important practice was adopted at the hospital: in order to maintain the expertise and vigilance of the physicians regarding medical questions and professional ethics, the medical staff convened from time to time for discussions. One evening they were discussing the morality of performing abortions. Jonah felt he could not bear the tension and pain that lodged within him when this question was discussed, but when he got up to leave the meeting, Aharon stopped him.

"Why aren't you staying?" he asked. "You look tired and tense." Jonah waved his arms in a gesture of despair. "Come on, we need these meetings. They help us to keep our humanity. You must not surrender to this dark mood."

Jonah relented and went back in. The discussion began with a report from one of the doctors. He told of hundreds of abortions performed in the past year. "We carry out all these difficult operations according to all the rules of medical science and adopt methods adapted to the limited means at our disposal. I must point out that we are able to prevent complications. Not a single death has been caused as a result of the surgical procedures we perform."

There was silence among the participants of the meeting. Jonah looked around. None of the doctors present in the room protested. He raised his hand, waved it in front of the speaker, and said, "You are subjugated to the murderous norms dictated by the Germans. You must not surrender to the brutality that commands you to commit these acts." Voices started to be heard in the crowded hall.

The speaker asked for silence and said in a loud voice, "In case of danger to the mother and her baby, medical ethics require saving the mother and sacrificing the fetus."

"All the Jews of the ghetto face a threat!" Jonah said. "Using medical science to claim that you are rescuing the mother and therefore are allowed to kill the fetus is immoral. A way must be found to circumvent this immoral argument."

Aharon looked in amazement at his friend, whose veins were now bulging from his pale forehead. Aharon approached Jonah and tried to calm him.

The speaker continued to defend the doctors' actions. "Even here in the ghetto, rabbis debated the question. Our rabbi, Ephraim Oshri, approved the abortions on the basis of Talmudic sources. Due to the mortal danger for the woman, she must be rescued, and termination of the pregnancy must be allowed."

"If we choose life," Jonah muttered, "we must find a way to resist this decree. This is the same choice the Israelites faced in Egypt when Pharoah declared: 'Every newborn son will be cast into the Nile.'" After citing this biblical verse, Jonah left, his head bowed.

As he walked across the hospital yard, he heard footsteps behind him and then his friend Aharon's voice. "Hey, Jonah! Wait for me. I want to talk to you." Jonah stopped. He had not said anything to Aharon about Tzila, but clearly his friend knew something was wrong.

"What's going on with you, my friend?" Aharon said. "I feel something is really bothering you."

"Tzila is pregnant!" Jonah blurted out. His friend smiled at him. "I have known for over a month," Jonah continued. "At first, I tried to persuade her to give it up, but she flatly refused. I must support her. The hope for a child keeps her alive."

Aharon paused, carefully choosing his words. "She's not the only one. There are other women who are fighting the ban. Does anyone else know?" he asked.

"So far no one, but my family is starting to suspect. I'll have to tell them."

When Jonah got home, he told Tzila about his conversation with Aharon.

Tzila spoke sadly: "I had a big quarrel with your sister Haya today. She asked me to bring a bucket of water. I was scared, so I told her I couldn't, and she started shouting, and again she called me a princess."

"It's time to tell them. We can't hide it anymore."

The following evening, Jonah gathered all the occupants of the hut. Haya did not stop fidgeting. Her nerves were frayed. Jonah feared her reaction but decided not to delay.

"Tzila is pregnant. That's why she's stopped working and is less helpful here. She needs to be careful. We've decided to keep the pregnancy and have the baby. We'll make all the necessary arrangements. I trust you not to tell anyone."

There was silence. Haya got up and started moving back and forth, slapping her hands on her thighs and making snarling noises. Sarah, the boarder who had recently joined them, approached her and held her softly. "Shh, shh, quiet."

It was the signal for everyone to speak up. "What will happen to us if they catch us?" asked Bracha, the cousin whose husband had disappeared two months before. "Is there not enough suffering around us? Why take the risk? It's not just you, it's all of us."

Jonah had prepared himself for such arguments. He had heard them many times before. But he let them voice their fears and then calmly explained: "Our plan is for Tzila to hide for the next few months, until the time of birth. Then we'll see what happens."

"It is better that we don't know what you're doing and what you're planning. The more we know, the more damage we might cause," Moshe said.

Jonah also shared his secret with Lazar, his cousin and best friend. Lazar was associated with the ghetto administration and belonged to a group of Jewish policemen. He was known among the ghetto people for his generosity.

When they were both alone, they would converse in Hebrew. It was a connecting link that gave them pleasure and created a space that enabled them to leave for other worlds, albeit just for a few moments. Jonah had anticipated Lazar's supportive response. His blue eyes were immediately filled with tears, accompanied by a smile, followed by a robust hug. Jonah told him about the recent chain of events, the deliberations, and the decision. Lazar replied, "Well, well, that's the right decision!" Then he paused a little and examined Jonah's face.

"It looks like there's something else you want to tell me, Lazar," Jonah said. "What are you thinking about?"

"Listen, Jonah, it's not enough just to plan how to keep the pregnancy and birth a secret. There is the baby's life afterward. It's very difficult to keep a baby here, I don't have to tell you."

"We're thinking about that too," Jonah interrupted his friend.

Lazar continued, "I want to share a secret with you. In my position, I hear things that do not reach the ears of others. More and more people are looking for ways to smuggle children out of the ghetto. We in the police cover for those who flee to the forests or join the partisans. You at the hospital also give the partisans medicine and bandages. Do you know why? There are rumors that the Russians are prevailing over the Nazi beasts. Perhaps the end of the war is near. If the Russians are advancing, the Nazis are going to be busy fighting and less concerned with us. Now, more Lithuanians are ready to hide Jewish children in their homes. After all the horrific things they've done, they are afraid of the Russians and want to prove that they are humane. We know that some mothers working in the brigade are coming to the city to look for people willing to help smuggle out their children."

Jonah listened. He knew Lazar was right. He himself had been asked to come to women's homes at dawn, before they went to work outside the ghetto, to inject their young children with anesthetics. When he left, he would notice a backpack at the ready to carry a drugged child out of the ghetto. He knew that he and Tzila would have to find their own way to get their child out of the ghetto.

"I know, Lazar. Thanks for the support. For now, I don't want to involve you in this. I'll look for a Lithuanian acquaintance and I'll talk to Tzila when the time comes."

Jonah worked out a plan. He knew that a lot of intelligence was passed from the ghetto and that forbidden goods were smuggled into it via the pharmacy carts run by the authorities to and from drug warehouses. Jonah had been out with the medicine cart before, but this time he was going to use it to make contact with friends outside who might agree to take their baby.

First, he needed to get in touch with a Lithuanian friend. But when he arrived at the friend's home, which he remembered because they used to have tea together at the patisserie next door, there was no trace of him. He knew better than to ask about him at the patisserie and instead headed back to the pharmacy. He would have to find another way.

Two weeks later, a plan came together. He was contacted by the family of a woman who had arrived at the hospital three years earlier in critical condition. Her family members were at her bedside, expecting her to die—but Jonah managed to bring the woman back to life. Forever grateful, they had learned of Jonah's situation and sent a note saying he should come to see them. At the appointed place, a pleasant-looking tall man was waiting for him. The man spoke: "Doctor, we cannot forget how good you were to us. We have already taken in a Jewish girl, so we asked my sister-in-law to help. She lives on a farm a hundred miles away. Your baby will be safe there."

Jonah asked, "Why are you doing this?"

"Doctor, we want to help you. We are people of faith. God commands us to be compassionate."

Jonah tucked his hand into his pocket, quickly undid the seam, and pulled out banknotes wrapped in a handkerchief. The man hurriedly shoved the bundle into his pocket.

Jonah shook his hand, tilted his hat so it shadowed his dark eyes, and hurried back to the ghetto. That day, he presented Tzila with his plan for the baby's hiding place. He told her about other cases in which children were hidden by Lithuanians. He assured her that all would be well and convinced her that life on a farm, without many neighbors, was a better option for Elida than trying to hide her in the ghetto, and that food and milk for their child would be more available on the farm. Jonah did not tell her about the children who sneaked back into the ghetto or were returned. Nor did he tell her that in other ghettos children were taken from their parents and killed. He did not mention that Aharon and his staff had recently helped an unmarried woman give birth and then put her baby in a large basket and placed him on the hospital doorstep. He did not tell his wife that the baby died ten days later from lack of milk.

THREE MONTHS LATER, ON A STORMY EVENING IN THE FALL of 1943, a baby girl was born to Jonah and Tzila. When the labor pains began, Haya ran to the hospital to alert Jonah, who promptly went to Aharon and whispered: "Please come to our hut in an hour or two." Aharon nodded. He understood.

Jonah had inconspicuously dug out a bunker (*malina*) at the back of the hut where Tzila could hide during her final months of pregnancy and where the newborn could be sheltered. The sound of the opening of the passage to the hideout signaled the arrival of Aharon, who hurried to check Tzila. "Just in time," he said. "The baby's head is crowning."

Tzila groaned and Jonah breathed with her. He moved with her every writhe. Tzila pushed and pushed, and then, finally, a baby squeezed between Tzila's thighs. "A princess!" Aharon announced. "A *meidele*," Jonah whispered. Aharon severed the umbilical cord. As in all the forbidden births in the ghetto, he could not ignore the symbolism of the act of disconnecting the baby from the mother.

Jonah held the little baby for a few seconds, and when she gave her first loud cry, Aharon remarked, "Stronger than usual." A cry of protest, Jonah thought, and he hurried to erase these thoughts from his mind.

He wrapped his daughter in a blanket. Aharon kept busy with delivering the placenta and stitching. When he was done, Jonah put the baby on Tzila's belly. Tzila burst into heavy sobs, and Jonah joined her, weeping bitterly too. "*Mein kind*, my child," they both cried in their mother tongue. Aharon patted Jonah on the shoulder and kissed Tzila. "Congratulations!" he said, and hurried back to the hospital.

IN THE FOLLOWING DAYS, TZILA NEVER LET HER DAUGHTER out of her arms. Jonah came and went and made sure Tzila's food was as healthful as possible. He asked those going out to the pharmacy to try to bring back an apple and some vegetables. "Tzila is sick," he explained, his face impassive. At the hospital, he continued to bandage the injured, drain wounds, and operate as often as resources allowed.

The rest of the time he spent planning to smuggle his daughter out of the ghetto. In the evenings, he sat on the straw mattress and showered kind words on Tzila and the baby, whom they had finally named Elida. The name—

"nonbirth" in Hebrew—conveyed the stark reality in which they lived: she was a "forbidden" daughter.

Jonah contacted the Christian family that had agreed to take Elida, and they made the final arrangements to smuggle the baby out of the ghetto. They needed to act quickly. An order had just been issued to remove thirty-five hundred Jews from the ghetto and transfer them to barracks on the outskirts of the city of Kovno, near the workplaces.

As the horizon became gloomier, there was a lot of tension at the hospital. Two senior doctors had disappeared. It was later learned that they had escaped from the ghetto. This posed great danger to the Jewish medical staff and leadership.

In the midst of these difficult days, Jonah initiated a meeting with Lazar and Aharon. "I need your help. I've arranged with a Lithuanian family to take our baby in two days. Since the hospital is near the gate, I arranged with them that I would turn on a light in the room on the second floor, to signal that everything is fine and that I am ready with the baby. Outside the ghetto, the farm woman will wait with her brother-in-law. They will stroll along the fence near the gate. I need one of you to be in the hospital. Aharon, will you do it?" Aharon nodded. He did not mention that he had helped to smuggle out another toddler a few days earlier. "Lazar, you will wait near the fence to make sure everything is okay, and we'll decide how to signal a warning if you notice anything." The three friends agreed.

"I have another matter for you, a very important one," Lazar told Jonah. "Since we don't know what will happen next and what our fate will be, I want us to assure each other that if either of us does not survive, the other or his spouse will take care of their child and raise them as if they were his own. We will be their parents and will love them as our own flesh and blood."

Jonah enfolded Lazar in a big hug, shook his hand, and in a trembling voice uttered an oath: "Your child is my child, my child is your child, and Aharon is our witness." In the sky, a yellow streak appeared in the space between two black clouds.

ON THE APPOINTED DAY, TZILA AND JONAH BEHAVED AS IF they were preparing a package for delivery. It was only when Jonah injected the Luminal into his daughter that he faltered for a moment, putting down the syringe and moving his fingers to release the tremor that had struck them. Tzila looked down. Elida was wrapped and placed in a basket. Tzila leaned over her daughter, kissed her closed eyes, and turned to face the wall. Jonah lingered, but Tzila asked him to go.

With heavy footsteps, Jonah carried the basket toward the hospital. He did not enter the usual way but circled the entrance plaza. Lazar was at the gate in his police uniform. He pretended to be patrolling as usual. In the hospital, only a few windows were lit. Jonah's office was located on the second floor, and its window, facing the back fence, was dark.

Aharon came out of his house as if by chance and met Jonah. "Is all well?" he asked. Jonah waved his hand as agreed. Aharon refrained from looking at the basket. Everything should look normal. Lazar, from where he stood, waved his hand. Jonah waved back at him.

A Lithuanian couple walked toward the fence. The tall, golden-haired woman was Stanislava, the sister of the patient Jonah had saved. She was accompanied by her brother-in-law, Sergei. A couple of lovers, people must have thought. Even the two German soldiers, who had just finished their shift and were still holding weapons in their hands, did not seem to suspect anything. If they had looked closely, they would have noticed that the couple's eyes occasionally turned toward the second floor of the hospital building to see if the light was on in the window at the corner.

"The light is on," Sergei whispered to Stanislava, and they proceeded toward the fence. "Wait, now it's off. Maybe something went wrong." Just as they were about to turn away, they saw the light turn on again—and then it went out a second time. "Something's wrong," he whispered again. "We'll have to run away. But no, look, it's on!" They waited a few minutes and this time the light did not go off. They hurried toward the fence.

The man on the other side of the fence wore a black coat and hat. He carried a package. "She'll sleep for many more hours," he whispered as he handed it over. "She's been given an anesthetic shot. Take care of her. Bless you!"

He lingered no more.

2

Rita, Childhood on the Farm

EVEN THOUGH IT WAS A CHILLY, CLEAR NIGHT, Stanislava's and Sergei's backs were awash with sweat. With the basket of dangerous cargo in their hands, they crossed the bridge.

They took the baby to the home of Stanislava's sister, Ivona, where she slept for many more hours. When Stanislava took off Elida's blanket and hat, she was startled by the tiny head covered in black curls. How different she looked from her daughter, Audra, and her sister's children.

Stanislava decided to call the baby by her middle name, Rita. The next afternoon, Stanislava said goodbye to Ivona and Sergei and left with Rita, who was again sedated with the medicine Jonah had given her. Stanislava laid the baby in the basket, covered her with a blanket, and boarded a train that would take them to the town of Siauliai, about a hundred and twenty miles away. From there, they would head to the family farm in Kelmuciai, near the village of Joniškis.

"I'm bringing you a big doll," Stanislava had told her daughter, Audra, who was already on the farm with her grandmother.

She placed the basket with the sleeping baby at her feet.

The passengers in the train were preoccupied with their packages and their own affairs. Except for one, a Lithuanian, who did not stop gaping and winking at her. She turned away from him and stared at the view through the dusty windows. Occasionally the train stopped. At one of the stations, all the passengers were asked to show their IDs to two German policemen. Stanislava adjusted the cover on the basket at her feet and showed her papers to the German with a seductive smile. He looked at her pretty face and not at the certificate.

"Where to?" he asked.

"I live in Siauliai," she replied flirtatiously.

The train stopped at another station and Stanislava worried: What if the baby wakes up? She did not trust the passengers on the train.

The reason for the delay was a train full of German soldiers passing on the main track. Some of the passengers clenched their fists. "When will it all be over?" she heard the neighbor on the adjacent bench whispering to the man next to her. "Then the Russians will be back. Will that be better?" the man asked her.

That man reminded her of her husband, Stefan, who had been gone for more than two years. Stefan, a member of the Lithuanian underground, was living with partisans in the forests.

She shivered as she wondered: What if Stefan decided to return to the farm and found Rita? He would not be happy that she had taken in a Jewish girl, unless he could think of a way to make money from it. But she knew that her mother, bless her Christian soul, would understand. She said to herself, "Mother always taught me to encourage kindness and compassion. Dr. Freidman helped Ivona, and we will take care of Rita. It's a good feeling to know that I'm saving a child in this evil world."

The train set off again with a shriek. As they approached Siauliai, Stanislava rearranged her packages. What is the correct way to hold the basket? And how should I carry the rest of the packages?

As they pulled in, she heard someone calling her name. "Stanislava, Stanislava!" A man's voice. In a panic she turned her head. Next to a truck stood an acquaintance of hers from the area.

"Where have you been, in Kovno?"

"Yes, with my sister."

"And what do you have in the basket? Give it to me, I'll help you."

"No, no, no need, maybe you can help me carry the packages lying here on the floor? I'm looking for a way to get to Joniškis."

"No problem," he said. "I'll take you in my truck. I just need to load a few crates of goods that came on the train." He pointed to a pile of sealed crates.

"I don't know," she replied hesitantly.

"What are you afraid of?"

"Nothing," she replied, and immediately smiled. "Okay, I'd love to come!"

"So come on up!" He tried to help and take the basket from her.

"It's tied tightly to my arm, it's okay."

"You probably have something very expensive there. What did you bring from Kovno?"

"Don't ask." She burst out laughing. "Women are not to be probed about their secrets."

"Okay, okay," he relented.

The truck started moving down the old road. Stanislava was afraid the baby would wake up with the truck's motion. She continued to hold on to the basket and started a loud conversation to cover up any crying. She giggled with the driver about Stefan, gossiped about the neighbors, answered his questions, and told him about what she had seen in Kovno.

When he asked a question about what had happened to all the Jews there, she evaded it.

"Who knows? What do I care? The main thing was that I was with my sister, where I rested a little. You know, a big city is better than being on the farm."

"Maybe," he replied, "but not in days of war."

They finally reached the center of the village. "I can bring you to your farm too."

"No, no need. Our farmhand is waiting here for me."

The horse and cart from the farm stood in the plaza. Next to them stood the faithful Yoshko, who had been with the family on the farm for several years.

Yoshko approached her and took the packages. She continued to hold the basket. "Quick, quick," she urged Yoshko, climbing onto the front seat and not letting go of the basket.

"Yoshko, you know what I have here, right? Mother told you?"

"Yes, yes." Yoshko smiled at her and glanced at the basket.

"Nobody is supposed to know about her. Do you understand? Ivona and Sergei let us take care of her. She will be with us, and no one is allowed to know. Only those who live on the farm know."

Yoshko nodded and confirmed enthusiastically.

Now Stanislava was breathing more easily. Her familiar and beloved landscape, her home. And she would see Audra very soon! After Kovno, the trains, the tension, and the barbed-wire fences, here was the winding road from Joniškis to the Kelmuciai farm, fields where puddles of water mirrored the movement of the clouds above and the bare trees planted in disorder. How good it was to live here!

Stanislava had inherited the farm in Kelmuciai from her father. The farm was located at the edge of the main road between Siauliai and northern Lithuania. It was indeed an isolated farm, but its proximity to a main road sometimes brought unwanted guests. Several times, German soldiers came in and demanded food from the farm. Lithuanian partisans also emerged from the forests and stole pigs and sheep at will.

How would she present the two girls as her daughters? After all, they looked so different. Audra was blond and blue-eyed, while Rita had curly black hair and dark eyes. Audra resembled her; everyone could see it right away. But Rita? Perhaps she could say that she was like her dad, who was not on the farm.

Audra and Stanislava's mother greeted them. The six-year-old ran to her, hugged her legs, and immediately asked, "Where is the doll you promised me?"

"You've never seen such a doll. Let's go inside."

At home, Stanislava placed the "doll" on Grandma's bed.

Audra was stunned. "It's not a doll, it's a baby!"

The baby burst into tears and the grandmother hurried to the kitchen and returned with a cup of milk she had prepared in advance. "Here, see how Mom feeds her, and then you may help. She will be your living doll."

Audra held her mother's hand and insisted on feeding Rita with her. The spoon was raised, and the baby sucked the liquid, some of which dripped down her chin and into the folds of her neck. She was hungry. The three women stood around and pursed their lips with each serving of the spoon.

"What shall we call her?" asked Audra, bouncing around the bed.

"Rita, her name is Rita! And she's going to be your little sister."

"And where is her mother?" the girl asked.

"Far, far away, and now she will live with us here."

Gradually, the excitement around the girl's arrival subsided. The grandmother took responsibility for the baby. She changed her, bathed her, and suggested to Stanislava that they cut her curls so that the black hair would not stand out. Life on the farm was back on track. Stanislava was busy managing the farm, selling produce in the nearby village, supervising the workers, and feeding the animals.

Ivona's son, Nijul, who was Audra's age, had recently been sent from Kovno to live with his grandmother on the farm.

One evening, as the family was having dinner and Rita was asleep in her basket, there was suddenly a muffled noise from outside. Stanislava got up, opened the window, and saw three German soldiers approaching the front door. They were laughing, and one of them pulled a gun out of his belt. She turned pale and waved at Grandma and at the basket. "Hurry, hurry, take her to the barn."

The grandmother grabbed the basket and hurried out the back door. There were loud knocks on the front door.

"Please, come in," Stanislava called and opened the door, smiling broadly.

The three entered the hot kitchen. One of them had a drawn gun. "Search!" they said in German.

"Please," Stanislava replied in German, "perhaps you would like to have some soup? We also have wine."

The soldier returned his pistol to his belt, and the three exchanged smiles. They sat down around the table and pounded their fists on it. "Let's go!"

"Mom," Audra asked, "why did Grandma go out with Rita?"

"Grandma was not feeling well," Stanislava replied to Audra, trying to indicate that she should keep quiet.

"What did she say?" asked one of the soldiers, immediately adding, "What a beautiful blond girl with blue eyes. Like ours."

"Thank you. This is my daughter, Audra, and this is Nijul, her cousin."

"Beautiful, beautiful! What did she say?"

"She was asking about my mother, who is not feeling well. We are letting her sleep. But don't worry, I will take good care of you."

Stanislava knew how to speak German and how to flirt. She danced around them, giggled, poured mulled wine into glasses, talked about the farm. When asked about her husband, she told them he'd been gone a long time.

"What a fool! With a woman like you?" said one of them, and put his hand on her waist. Stanislava shook him off.

"Well, we have to go," said one of the soldiers. His cheeks were red. "We will come again," he said with a smile.

"Please, please do," she replied. The smile muscles on her face ached. "You can always get soup and wine here."

"And a beautiful woman!" said the enthusiastic soldier.

From that evening on, the shutter of the window facing the main road was always open, so that the German officers who might choose to stop at the farm could be observed in advance.

It was harder when neighbors from adjacent farms came to visit. In those cases, Grandma and the older children had to stay and entertain. Only Rita would disappear, usually out back to pick vegetables with Stanislava. On Sundays, Rita would remain on the farm with Yoshko while the rest of the family attended church services in the nearby village.

Rita got used to the farm. She crawled among the animals, listened to Lithuanian songs, and clapped her hands when asked. Her black curls were trimmed every week.

Stanislava sometimes thought of Rita's parents. If only she could tell Rita's mother how big her daughter had grown.

One day, a friend from a nearby village returned from Kovno with a letter from Ivona. In the letter, she reported what was happening in Kovno and sent an additional amount of money that came from Rita's parents for her custody. In the letter, Ivona suggested that Stanislava come to Kovno for a few days. "Do not bring Nijul," she wrote. "It's not quiet here. There are bombings."

In late April, Stanislava traveled to Kovno. The city had become grayer. Sandbags had been placed on every street corner. Some of the houses in the city center were demolished. At night, the windows were darkened. The Jewish girl who had been living at Ivona and Sergei's home had been sent off with the nanny to take refuge in the nanny's village. Ivona and Sergei could no longer keep her in Kovno. The neighbors had begun to be suspicious.

"The Jews there in the ghetto, I don't know how they keep going," Ivona told Stanislava in a whisper when they were alone at home. "A few weeks ago, we saw trucks with a lot of German soldiers heading to the ghetto. The bridge was packed with their army. There were endless shootings all day, and in the evening we saw soldiers leading people and children to the fort. The soldiers pushed them, shouted at them. There were also trucks crossing the bridge with children. The next day, they returned empty."

"Did you see all that?" Stanislava asked in horror.

"Yes, in the morning when I went to work at the factory. Many of the workers from the ghetto no longer come to work. Those who do, the poor women, cry ceaselessly. It's hard to look at them. I've heard horrible things, how they snatched the children from their hands, tied the children, and threw them onto the trucks. There is talk that soon there will be no Jews here at all."

"I wonder if Rita's parents are still alive," Stanislava said.

"Yes, they are alive," Ivona replied. "That's why I called you. I got a note from the phone operator at the factory that the doctor and his wife wanted to know what was going on with their girl. And the girl's mother asked if you could meet with her."

"I know it's important to tell them that the girl is safe with us, but now I understand that it's really dangerous to meet. I'm scared. What if they follow her? I can't have them see me talking to her."

"I don't think they would take that risk. Dr. Freidman is so careful. If it were not possible, they would not have suggested meeting you."

The next day, Ivona returned from work with clear instructions for Stanislava. They would meet in two days at the women's bathhouse, a popular meeting place since many homes had no means of heating water for baths. Only Rita's mother, Tzila, would come. Stanislava provided details that would make it easier to identify her.

They were to meet at the entrance. Women of all ages with bags and baskets were lined up there. Stanislava surveyed the arriving women and was afraid to stand there for a long time. One should be careful of any unusual movement. She stood in line, occasionally turning her head back. Soon her turn would come and there was no sign of the doctor's wife. She decided to get out of the queue, stood aside, and began rummaging through her bag. Suddenly, she saw a skinny woman in an oversized gray coat. Her hair was braided and pinned to her head. Despite the grayness of her appearance, the woman walked in a slow and elegant manner. In her hand, she held a basket similar in size and color to the basket that had once contained Rita. That was the prearranged sign. Tzila approached her immediately, hugged her, and said to her in Lithuanian, "Sister, how glad I am to see you." They joined hands, waited for their turn, and stepped inside.

Surrounded by women of all ages, in the midst of the bustle and steaming fumes, they could talk undetected. After taking off their clothes, they clambered into a wooden barrel full of water, and there Stanislava told Tzila about Rita.

"You have nothing to worry about. Your child is safe with us. She's already standing and crawling a lot. She eats well. You know that it's easier to get food on the farm than in the city. She also sleeps well. My daughter, Audra, loves her. Everything is fine. Here, the war will be over soon, the Russians are nearing." Tzila did not let her finish. She burst into tears and fell on Stanislava's neck.

"We have to be careful," Stanislava whispered.

"Yes, yes," Tzila replied. She moved away a little and now only clasped Stanislava's hands. "I don't know how to thank you. You saved my daughter. It's only thanks to you that I am alive! Do you know about the *Kinderaktion*? What the damned Nazis did to the ghetto children? There are no more children in the ghetto." She burst into tears again. "They took them all and killed them, Moishele and Pini and Mano, the children of our family, and all the elders too."

"Let's go," Stanislava urged her. She felt uncomfortable. "We must not draw attention to ourselves. Let's meet again on the bench out there," she said, pointing to it.

Tzila climbed out of the water, got dressed, and walked a short distance behind this stranger, in whose care she had entrusted her daughter. Would she ever get to see Elida again? Would she meet her little daughter again? If only they would let her hug her child one more time.

On the bench, the women combed and braided each other's hair. "You're our guardian angel," Tzila told Stanislava. "I know that if my daughter had stayed with me, neither she nor I would be alive anymore."

"You know, Rita has eyes like yours, big and brown. She really loves the animals on our farm," Stanislava said, changing the subject.

Tzila stared for a few more moments and then suddenly the tears disappeared. She gathered herself up, kissed Stanislava's flushed cheeks, tucked a tin box in her hands, and without turning her head, walked toward the exit. Stanislava carefully placed the tin box in the basket. She glanced around, took her basket, and left the bathhouse.

"How wretched and how brave Rita's mother is," she later told her sister.

WHEN SPRING ARRIVED IN MAY 1944, THE ANIMALS WERE taken out of the barns, huts, and winter cages, and Audra and Nijul ran among the snorting pigs and screaming birds that roamed the yard. Rita took her first steps and tried to keep up with the children. She fell and cried but then calmed down and tried again.

In the evening, when Rita was asleep and Stanislava and her mother were sitting in the kitchen, the grandmother tried to persuade her daughter to baptize Rita. "It'll be better for her. She won't feel any different and we won't have to hide her from the neighbors. I watched her today, a little girl who doesn't laugh out loud."

"And if we baptize her, will she laugh? We have no permission to do so. I promised her parents that she'd be raised as a Jew. If they come to get her, what will I tell them?"

"Do you think there's a chance of that? You know there are almost no Jews left in Lithuania anymore. Ivona says that every day they hear gunshots at the Ninth Fort and trucks and trains take the Jews out."

"I made a commitment to Dr. Freidman and his wife. We'll wait patiently." The two did not notice Audra come in and sit by the stove, until she suddenly asked, "Mom, what are Jews?"

They exchanged glances. "There are things I cannot explain to you now," Stanislava told her. "Don't talk to anyone about Jews. You're already a big girl. You need to know that this word must not be mentioned."

"If the war ends, will Dad come back to us? Will Nijul return to Kovno to Aunt Ivona? Will they take Rita?"

"Audra, you're asking too many questions. Go to bed, it's late!"

In early July 1944, the roads in the area were crowded with Red Army convoys heading for Kovno and the Baltic coast. Carts laden with equipment and families of refugees moved along the roads. There was restlessness on the farm.

Someone said he saw Stefan with a group of nationalists in the area. Stanislava was afraid to leave the farm with her mother and children. On Sundays, when they went to church, she started taking Rita with her.

The pastor always greeted them happily. He stroked Rita's head, and this gesture confirmed that the girl had joined the family. Stanislava's neighbors acted that way too.

Stanislava set up a stall selling vegetables, milk, and cheese made on the farm on the nearby road. She hoped that the refugees and soldiers would buy the produce from her for a few coins so she could continue to maintain the farm. Each evening, she counted the meager amount she earned. "People have no money," she complained to her mother. She did not tell her how the Russian soldiers had tried to kiss her and reach for her breasts and how half of the produce was snatched away without payment. At the end of the day, she made sure the doors were tightly sealed.

One Sunday at church, she heard her neighbors talking about the annihilation of the Jews. "Enough, there are no more Jews in Lithuania, neither in Siauliai nor in Vilna and Kovno. The Germans blew up the ghetto in Kovno. Some of the Jews were taken by train to Germany."

A shudder went through her. "What's the matter, Stanislava, are you unwell? Should we bring you water?"

"I'm all right," she said. "I'm just tired. I want to sit down." A few minutes later she called Audra and her mother and said, "Let's return to the farm!"

A few days later, Ivona came to the farm and confirmed

the rumors. "Before the Germans left, they blew up the ghetto. The entire hospital was destroyed. They trucked out all the Jews who remained in the ghetto. Those who survived because they were outside the ghetto are roaming the streets of Kovno, looking for relatives." There was no word of Dr. Freidman.

WINTER KNOCKED ON THE PEASANTS' DOORS. THE ROADS were rough, flooded with refugees, Russian soldiers, and Lithuanian nationalists who continued to rob farmers of their produce. Stanislava and her family hardly managed to stay alive, let alone make any money standing in rags with their goods on the road. Only the children went on with their routine. Audra played games with Rita, taught her to speak, laughed when Rita cooperated, and got angry when Rita sat in the corner and followed the grandmother with her eyes. Rita regularly greeted Stanislava with laughter and hugs.

In January 1945, the Russians reached the Baltic Sea and annexed all of Lithuania to the Soviet Union. And suddenly, with no prior notice, Stefan arrived at the farm one Sunday morning.

As the family members were eating their porridge before church, they heard squeaking shoes on the snowy path. The dogs in the barn barked. Stanislava glanced at her mother, who picked up Rita and went into the back wing. There was silence behind the front door.

"Who's there?" Stanislava asked quietly in Lithuanian, then in Russian, and opened the door slightly.

A man's foot in a muddy boot was stuck in the doorway. "It's me!" Stefan hollered and burst in. "Where's my beautiful wife?" He wrapped his arms around Stanislava. "How 'bout a kiss, woman, where's a kiss?" he bellowed. "And where's my Audra?"

Audra jumped to her feet and with her eyes asked permission from her mother to run to her father, whom she had not seen for a long time.

"Come!" he roared. "You're as beautiful as your mother. How you've grown up! Eating well, eh? What is this? Nijul's here? You're eating well too?"

"Yes, sir, I'm here because of the war."

"War, eh? The Germans exit, the Russians enter, what?"

Stefan sat down at the table. "Where do you get so much food?"

"It's not much. I work hard for it," Stanislava said, and hurried to serve him a bowl of porridge.

"Where's your mother?" Stefan growled. "Oh, here's our babushka. What about a hug for your son-in-law?"

The grandmother straightened her headscarf. "Hello, Stefan. You're back home at last."

"Dad, we have a little sister! Grandma, where's Rita?"

"Sister, eh? Never call a dirty Jew a sister!" Stefan bellowed, his face turning cold. "Think I don't know everything? You think I haven't heard about the Jewish girl? You got money for her, woman. That's why you have food.

Now there are no more Jews, and this girl will not be in my house!"

Stanislava cringed, and Grandma's lips began to tremble. Audra and Nijul watched it all in horror.

"Where is the little Jew girl? Bring her to me and I'll show you what to do with Jews!"

"You will not touch her!" Stanislava screamed at him. "Stefan, please, we'll fix everything. We need to talk. Mom, go to church with the kids and I'll stay with you here and talk."

"Does the Jew also go to church?"

"Our good pastor already knows about her and so do some of the neighbors."

Once the children were gone, Stefan felt reassured by the silence of the house. His wife, whose beauty had not been diminished by years of war and hard work, was now within reach. The story with the Jewess could wait.

Two hours later, with the family about to return from church, Stanislava finally returned to the subject of Rita. "If you're thinking of staying here, you'll have to accept Rita," she told Stefan. "You know I already got money for her and now they say that whoever took care of Jewish children during the war will get additional money for them. You can also give them away for a payment." Knowing her husband, she made sure she emphasized the financial benefits of the situation.

A few months later, Stefan disappeared for several weeks. Someone told Stanislava that he was involved in an attack on the Russians, was caught, and was sent to Siberia with a group of Lithuanian rebels. In July, Ivona came to take Nijul back to Kovno. In the evening, the two sisters sat and talked. "The city is in ruins," Ivona told Stanislava. "We haven't decided what to do. Sergei is afraid of the Russians, who are looking for Lithuanian soldiers. There are informants who already told them he was an officer in the Lithuanian army. We probably won't stay in Kovno."

"And what about the Jews?" Stanislava asked. "Do you think there's anyone left to wait for? What do we do with Rita and what about the other children who are on the farms? I've heard of several other families in the area who have taken in Jewish children."

"Come to Kovno. An orphanage for Jewish children has opened there. Occasionally, Jewish refugees come to look for their children. I heard that families with Jewish children are given money and food stamps there."

"Do you think there's a chance Dr. Freidman will come back?" asked the grandmother while peeling potatoes.

"No," said Ivona, lowering her voice. "They must have died when the ghetto was blown up. If they were alive, they would have found their way here. I suggest you come to Kovno and try to talk to people who might have known them."

Only later did they learn the details of what had happened. On July 8, 1944, as the Red Army approached Kovno, the Germans rounded up the Jews and transported them by train to camps in Germany—the men to Dachau and the women to Stutthof. Some of the ghetto residents chose to hide. Some were discovered and evacuated, while those who stayed below in the hideaways were eliminated by the Germans, who set fire to many houses in the ghetto. Jonah was in the hospital that day, and Tzila had joined him. The Germans blew up the ghetto hospital building, and neither Jonah nor Tzila survived.

IN THE SUMMER OF 1945, THE SKY WAS CLEAR, BUT DESTRUCTION, devastation, and pain were everywhere. The farms were in ruins. Families of refugees and survivors from Russia sought a safe haven, begging for bread and labor. Stanislava, like her farming neighbors, knew that Russia's victory and Lithuania's annexation to the Soviet Union would rob her of everything she had left.

She and her mother fought for survival that summer. Russian officials appeared and registered the family property. The whole area was declared a *kolkhoz,* a collective farm. Few animals remained on the farm, and most of the produce had to be sold through a collective marketing system. Stanislava tried to sell privately whatever remained. The grandmother was entrusted with growing the vegetables, milking, and processing dairy products, while Rita stayed with her. She got used to not interrupting. She would sit quietly in the corner of the barn and build towers from haystacks. At home, she took out the few books that were left and flipped through them. When Audra came home from school, Rita pulled her to the book corner and demanded that she tell her a story. Stanislava and her mother were very concerned about Rita's loneliness and the great responsibility of raising her.

"We'll have to decide what to do with the girl," said the grandmother. "She can't go on like this, alone and without a future. Today I saw her standing at the gate and crying. When I asked her what had happened, she whimpered that she was looking for you and Audra. You have to decide what to do. If we decide to keep her, we'll have to baptize her as a Christian. Otherwise, we'll need to give her away to the returning Jews."

"I know, Mama, but this is difficult for me. I feel sorry for her, and Audra is happy with her too. I cannot break my promise to her parents that she will remain Jewish. The picture of her mother crying in the bathhouse stays with me."

One evening, she said to her mother, "You know there are a lot of Russian refugees in Joniškis. Today, on the way to work I met a family, a mother with three children; the girls were about the same age as Audra. They were at the station, skinny and barely standing on their feet. They begged for a piece of bread."

"So, did you give them some bread?"

"Of course. They pounced on the food. I waited for them to finish and talked to the mother, whose name is Tanya. They are Russian refugees, who fled because of starvation. Their village near the border was completely destroyed in the war and they decided to stay in the area. They are tired of wandering."

"What have you promised them?" her mother asked, suspicious.

"Well, Mother," Stanislava replied, "you know how officials are now sending refugees to the farms? So, it's just a question of time until a refugee family is assigned to us. I'm thinking, then: Why not invite this family? The mother and children seem nice. I'd rather have a nice family we know a little bit than have to take refugees someone else has chosen for us."

AND SO, THE RUSSIAN REFUGEES CAME TO LIVE ON THE farm. At first, they cheered everyone up. The children frolicked in the fields all day. In the evenings, they prepared plays, hanging a sheet as a curtain, passing out instructions, and having fun. But sometimes things went wrong. One evening, only the children remained in the kitchen. A boiling pot had just been taken off the stove. Rita, who was demonstrating a new dance step that Audra had taught her, bumped into the pot and its boiling contents splashed down Rita's legs. Her cries summoned Stanislava to the kitchen. She deftly laid the girl down, beat egg yolks, and applied them to Rita's legs and buttocks. That evening, the show did not go on.

One other evening, Tanya, the Russian mother, asked Stanislava, "What are you going to do with Rita? Obviously, the girl is very attached to you. She's constantly checking with you and demanding your attention. She feels her difference. Either adopt her or let her go. The longer you postpone it, the harder the separation will be for both you and the girl."

Stanislava sighed. "We are all very attached to her, but I promised her father that she would grow up as a Jew. The poor man could not have known that the war would end this way. I have a box her mother gave me. It has pictures and letters in it and maybe they can provide some clues about surviving family members. I hid it—but maybe I should take a look."

That night she had a dream: She was with Rita and Audra at the train station in Kovno and was constantly walking between the platform and the station. Every time she was on the platform, a freight train passed, and she noticed Dr. Freidman, or Tzila combing her hair, through the iron bars of a black-painted carriage. Suddenly, Rita and Audra disappeared. She let out a scream and woke up drenched in sweat. She got out of bed, put on a thick sweater, lit a lantern, and began to look for the box. She finally found it hidden behind the icon. Inside it was a necklace with a Star of David and an engraving. On one side there were words in the language of the Jews and on the other side the girl's name was engraved in Lithuanian: Elida. There was also a page written by Dr. Freidman in Lithuanian requesting that the girl be raised as a Jew and stating: "If Tzila and I are not able to come to take her back, we ask that she be delivered to one of the Goldbergs in the following list." The first name was Lazar Goldberg. Alternative addresses were for Perla Frenkel, Tzila's sister in Tel Aviv, and Jonah Freidman's sisters, Leah Spiegel in Haifa and Sarah Itman in Toronto.

There were photographs at the bottom of the box. She spread them out in a row: a sixteen-year-old girl in a dark dress and braids, Tzila. Rita looks like her, Stanislava thought. And here are both parents, a young, good-looking, happy couple. There were also some pictures of Dr. Freidman in the hospital, wearing a white robe during surgery.

"I must write to the family," Stanislava said.

DURING THE WINTER MONTHS AND TOWARD THE SPRING, the residents of the Kelmuciai farm strained under the burden of the new Soviet government decrees. Stanislava, looking for ways to alleviate the family's financial distress, remembered that Ivona had suggested that she come to Kovno and contact the association that helped families who had hidden Jewish children.

Kovno looked like a wounded animal, licking its wounds. Groups of workers stood by ruined buildings and cleared piles of concrete and dirt. People with their heads bowed, wrapped in their heavy clothes, passed by in the street. Ivona had obtained the address of the Jewish orphanage for her. Arriving there, Stanislava saw Lithuanian women of different ages, some holding small children in their arms. It was evident that the children were not their own.

A Lithuanian woman of Stanislava's age started talking to her. "Are you hiding a Jewish girl?" she asked Stanislava. "I'm taking care of one. Do you know that you can get money for her? If I give her to the orphanage, they will pay me."

"And do you want to give her away?" Stanislava asked.

"I'm having a hard time with her," the woman said. "My husband demands that I hand her over, but I don't want to give her away just like that."

Stanislava, for her part, held back on information. She was used to hiding things.

A thin woman with short brown hair invited her into the room. "My name is Sarah Neshamit," she said. "I'm here to deal with the issue of Jewish children, orphans whose parents were killed in the war." She looked warmly at Stanislava and inspired her trust.

Stanislava explained the situation: "I'm willing to keep the girl, but the financial stress is enormous. And I promised her father . . ."

Sarah pulled out a sheet of paper and began asking questions: the names of Rita's parents, estimated date of birth, whether she knew for sure that her parents were murdered in the ghetto, whether she knew any relatives in Lithuania, and whether she had contacted them. "You understand that we need to check all the details in case a family member comes looking for her."

Stanislava chose not to tell her about the addresses she'd found in the box.

"Thank you for the courage you've shown and your kindness in saving Rita. God will reward you for your good deed. We appreciate it. People like you are the hope we have left after the hell we've experienced." She paused for a few seconds, looked into Stanislava's eyes, and touched her hand softly. "We now need to find out from our lists if Rita has family members, relatives who will come to look for her. You know that every day refugees come to us looking for and giving testimonies about other people. Before we decide, we need to know further details and facts."

"And in the meantime?" Stanislava asked. "I don't want to give her away yet. She can continue to live with me, but I need financial help and registration for her."

"I cannot decide alone," Sarah replied. "We need to find out everything. Whatever is decided, we'll let you know soon. And thank you again. There are not enough words to thank you. Don't worry, we'll be in touch with you."

Stanislava left the meeting disappointed. Despite Sarah's kindness, she did not believe that the people here could help her. When you hear "we," it usually means that no one takes responsibility. She would have to act in her own independent ways.

Ivona, hearing about the meeting, did not agree with her sister. "Sarah is right. Jewish survivors are returning to find family members here. They have their own ways of knowing. They need to check. And as for the money, who knows? Maybe you should contact the relatives you have on the list?" So, at the beginning of the New Year, Stanislava sent letters to the addresses on Jonah's list. She was careful not to write details that the censors might erase.

It took a few months, but letters and postcards began to arrive. The first letter was from Tzila's sister, Perla Frenkel, who confirmed the worst about Jonah and Tzila and thanked her for taking in the baby. There was also a letter from Leah, Jonah's sister, who lived in Haifa:

> *It's hard to believe that there are still good people like you and your family in our monstrous world. You and your family risked your lives to save a Jewish girl from the preying claws of a monster.*

There were also packages of clothes and gifts for Rita and for Audra. Rita received a doll that she never let go of from the moment it arrived. All she understood and knew was that the doll came from an aunt who lived far away. The packages also contained canned food and chocolate. These packages kindled great joy on the farm.

After Stanislava's visit to Kovno, Ivona came to the farm and told her that the Soviet authorities considered the Jewish rescue organizations dangerous, and that they had been forced to close their offices and leave Lithuania. Sarah, the woman Stanislava had met, was now in Poland. Ivona began to put pressure on Stanislava to make a decision soon.

Then Samuel Peipertas appeared on the farm. He had introduced himself in a postcard earlier as a Lithuanian

Jew who knew she was keeping a Jewish girl. Naturally, Stanislava was suspicious. Who was hiding behind this letter? Lithuanian extremists? Mean neighbors? Who had informed him about Rita? She showed the letter to her mother and Tanya. The women went over the text again and again. "The man is polite," Tanya stated. "He understands that he needs your cooperation."

So Stanislava, still cautious, allowed him to come to the farm. Peipertas was a tall man with thick eyebrows above his dark eyes and a snub nose. He wore a jacket, and his hair was pulled back. He had a captivating smile and handed Audra a bag of sweets. "They're for you and for Rita; go and share them with her." Audra rejoiced and ran to share the marmalade candies with Rita.

Peipertas revealed his intentions regarding Rita step by step. First, he told Stanislava about himself. "I was born in Krekenava, and when the Germans arrived, I moved to the Soviet side and enlisted in the Red Army. I fought with the Lithuanian division until I was wounded," he said, pointing to his disfigured hand. "I was devastated, but today the situation is better. When I was wounded and could no longer fight, I was released. The Red Army was already close to Vilna. Together with other Jews, we advanced into Lithuania to return home and meet the family. I already knew I wouldn't find them all, but I had hoped I might find at least a few of them. But no one was left.

"My Jewish friends and I are working every day to find Jewish children who were hidden by good people like you," he continued. "We do this for the children and their parents.

We have a sacred mission to give our people their lives and future back."

But Stanislava was not convinced. "I'm a simple woman. You talk about great issues that are important to you, but I don't think I can give away a girl who's like a daughter to me to someone who doesn't talk about what's good for the girl. I think it's best for her to stay with us."

Peipertas replied: "I came today just to get acquainted. There's no need to make any decisions either today or tomorrow or even next month. I promise not to do anything without your consent. I want you to trust me. I want what's best for Rita."

Stanislava softened. Peipertas then told her it was customary to pay families who had sheltered Jews. While Stanislava had no expectations, she was interested. "How much money are we talking about?" she asked.

"We're talking about a considerable amount of money," he replied.

But Stanislava could not give Rita up.

THEN, IN SEPTEMBER 1946, A POSTCARD ARRIVED FROM A Mr. Berke Goldberg of Vilna:

> *I'm Dr. Freidman's cousin. I learned that his daughter Elida (Rita) was staying with you. I don't know where she is now. I'd be grateful if you could let me know her whereabouts because I'd like to bring her here to live with us.*

The postcard shook Stanislava. She held it with a clenched fist, read it over and over again. Goldberg! This name appeared on Dr. Freidman's list. But was he to be trusted?

She decided to consult Peipertas. When he arrived and read the postcard, he frowned. "Have you made a decision about handing over Rita?"

She began to stammer, "I'm still undecided."

"Write to him," Peipertas advised cautiously. "Tell him that the girl is with you, that she's very much loved by the family and feels good and safe with you. Regarding her transfer, write that you wish to meet and get to know him. Tell him that other people, his people, are interested in her."

Stanislava replied to Goldberg:

> *I have the girl with me. She has a loving home that takes care of all her needs. I haven't decided whether to keep her with me, even though there are Jews who have offered to accept her and are willing to pay the amount of money that I deserve for all the years she has grown up with me and for the many expenses.*

Berke was not pleased with the reply and went to the farm, where he immediately noticed a little girl with cropped hair, dressed in rags, standing in the center of a small flock of geese. He had no doubt she was Elida. The resemblance to Jonah overwhelmed him, and he burst into tears. Rita watched the man standing and crying, and fled from him, calling desperately for Grandma.

Still, Stanislava was unmoved. The girl had been with the family for over three years, and it was going to be hard for them to separate. She told Berke again, as she had written to him, that she had already been approached about handing over Rita and was still undecided. Then she mentioned that she expected the payment to which Peipertas had said she was entitled.

Berke replied: "I came to take the girl and return her to her family. That was her parents' request. I don't have the required amount of money. Maybe I can raise some of it from the family and from Jews in Vilna. Please wait, don't give the girl to anyone. I'll return and pay you for everything you've done."

Meanwhile, the situation on the farm worsened by the day. Stanislava was even more convinced that she had to find an appropriate placement for Rita—and soon. Perhaps sensing that something was about to happen, Rita began clinging to Stanislava. When she was alone, she went to Stanislava's jewelry box, pulled out the cross pendant, and placed it around her neck. She mimicked Grandma's genuflection, gently kissed the cross, and placed it on the doll she had received as a gift.

To strengthen her position in the house, she tried to sweep the kitchen or drag a bucket of water from the water cistern in the yard to the house. She would sit next to the few books in the house and urge Audra to tell her stories.

"Mom, look, Rita already knows how to write her name!" Audra boasted.

"It's no wonder," the grandmother said. "Her father and mother were clever. The father was a doctor!"

During all these months, the correspondence between Peipertas and Stanislava continued. In September 1947, he wrote to her:

> *I've finally found what we've been looking for. I met a very nice Jewish couple who are suitable for taking care of Rita. Their last name is Rubin. They are Jewish refugees who spent the war years in Russia. Now they intend to settle in Vilna. They have no other children and will never have any. The man is a tailor, and the woman is younger than him. I showed them your pictures and they want to take in a Jewish girl like Rita and give her a home. They also have the amount required to pay you. They want you to come to Vilna with Rita to get acquainted and be together for a few days so that Rita gets used to it. I'll be there with all of you.*

Thus, the decision was made. The certainty of Rita's leaving Kelmuciai shook Stanislava and the rest of the family. She debated what to tell Rita. Should I tell her before the trip? What if it doesn't work out? Should I take the box with the photos that I received from Tzila? And how will Rita manage without Grandma, who is so attached to her? And how will Audra live without her "little sister"?

Her apprehension intensified as the day of the trip approached. Stanislava decided that Audra would also join them.

On their last night together on the farm, Stanislava crossed herself kneeling by her bed. She prayed for herself, for Audra, and for her mother, and asked God to help Rita succeed in her new life. Maybe one day Rita would thank her for this decision.

In the doorway, the grandmother hugged Rita tightly and handed her the rolls she had baked. The wagon brought them to Joniškis, where they boarded a truck to Siauliai. From there, they caught a train to Vilna, where Peipertas was waiting for them. He happily tossed Rita in the air. Rita kicked her legs a bit and asked him to take Audra instead of her.

Peipertas fulfilled his promise. He stayed with them for the three days they were in Vilna. They went to meet the Ruhin family at an acquaintance's house. When they arrived, Yocheved and Joel Ruhin were already at the apartment. Yocheved was a good-looking woman with wavy black hair, and Joel was bald and smiling. Yocheved took Rita's clenched hand. "Come, come here," she said. "How nice you are, what a beautiful dress you have."

Rita said nothing.

Yocheved tried again: "Come. I'm *Mame* [Mom] and here's *Tate* [Dad]." She pointed to Joel.

I would burst into tears if I were her, Stanislava thought to herself. Rita just clung to Stanislava.

"Why is she telling our Rita that she's her mother?" Audra asked.

No one had an answer.

That night, Rita, Audra, and Stanislava were left to stay in the apartment with the Ruhin couple. Rita calmed down when she realized she would be sleeping with Stanislava. A bed was prepared in the main room and the two girls fell asleep immediately, cuddling against Stanislava on each side.

The next day, the group walked through the streets of Vilna. This time they made their way to a photographer. The photographer seated the women, while the girls sat on their knees. On the left Yocheved, Rita's new mother, sat embracing Rita, and on the right Stanislava sat, her hand placed on Audra's shoulder. Above them, Joel stood next to Yocheved and Rita, while Peipertas stood on Stanislava's side, his hand on Audra's shoulder too. Two families united in one picture. The photographer tried to elicit a smile from them all, but only a slight smile appears on Stanislava's face. All the others seemed to be looking beyond the lens, a touch of astonishment or sadness on their faces.

When it was time to say goodbye, Stanislava unpacked her suitcase and handed over Rita's bundle of clothes. Though it was not yet winter, she took out Audra's old coat, which would now surely fit Rita, and a hat the grandmother had knitted for her. Rita watched Stanislava and said nothing.

"Her silence is harder for me than crying," Stanislava told Peipertas.

I wish they could give her the drops she got when I took her as a baby, Stanislava thought. If she slept, she would not see me and Audra leaving her. She knelt beside Rita, looked into her big brown eyes, and told her, "You will be fine with your new family. They are now your mother and father. Audra and I will come to visit you soon."

She hugged Rita, who did not resist or cry. Rita just looked longingly at Audra, who gave her a farewell hug and then quickly grabbed her mother's hand. After leaving the apartment, Stanislava felt as if her heart were beating backward: all the blood drained to her heavy feet as she walked. She felt Dr. Freidman's eyes piercing her back, as he silently held his hat behind the ghetto fence.

At the train station, Peipertas took Stanislava's hands, and when he was sure they were alone and that no one was near, he gave her Rita's redemption money. "I won't say goodbye now," he said. "I'll come to visit. In the meantime, there are more girls and boys waiting for me."

Samuel Peipertas never again came to visit Stanislava. A few weeks after Rita's transfer, he found another Jewish girl living on one of the farms in the area. He negotiated with the farmer about the amount of money he would receive for handing over the girl. When Peipertas returned, a group of Lithuanian nationalists were waiting for him, grabbed him, beheaded him, and threw his body into a well. Stanislava found out about it only later.

In September 1947, Berke Goldberg came back to the farm with the money he had raised to redeem Elida, to return her to her father's family. Flushed, Stanislava told him that the girl was no longer with her and that she was living with a good Jewish family in Vilna. He cried out in despair. She tried to calm him by giving him the address of the Ruhin family and suggesting that he could visit them anytime he wanted.

Berke Goldberg returned to Vilna feeling devastated. And what's more, his attempts to contact the Ruhin family failed. Eventually the Ruhins asked the Goldbergs to stop trying to contact them. They did not want their daughter to know that they were not her real family.

3

Gita Rubin, Vilna

Rita's new parents immediately changed her name to Gita, and she was instructed to call this new woman *Mame*. Rita could not understand why she had to do that, and she did not understand why she couldn't see Audra or Stanislava. She wanted to sit on Grandma's lap in the kitchen and run after the geese in the yard. She did not understand why the woman was saying strange words to her.

"Gita, Gitale," Yocheved called her in the first days.

"Rita," the girl murmured quietly. "I am Rita."

"Your name is Gita, I'm your mame, and that's your tate."

Yocheved looked pleadingly at her husband, who clearly wanted no part of any of this. He sat on the couch and stared and then said quietly, "This is your girl. I only agreed because you wanted this so much. But no child, no one, can replace my Duvidl."

In the weeks and months that followed, Gitale continued to stand by the window. She dragged the stool from the kitchen and stood on it. Only after she was scolded and spanked for trying to climb to the window did she learn to recognize these words: "You'll fall! It's forbidden!" Words like "forbidden!" "eat!" "come!" "bad girl!" were spoken in an angry voice, but sometimes they also said "good girl" or "delicious" or "our girl" to her.

When they went out into the street, she heard a familiar language. She turned and watched girls who looked like Audra and talked like her. In the courtyard and in the adjacent lot were boys and girls talking like Mame Yocheved and her new father.

"We speak Yiddish," Yocheved explained to her, "and the children who speak Yiddish are like us, Jews." She played in the yard with the children who lived in the same building. At first, she looked for animals outside, but very quickly realized that there were no geese here, no pig that could be petted on its wet nose. There was also no hay to roll in.

She did love going to the main street with Mame, who held her hand tightly as they went to buy bread from the baker and vegetables from an old woman who had lost almost all her teeth. Mame would examine every potato she picked from the long table strewn with cabbage heads and other vegetables. Gita would close her eyes and imagine Stanislava bending over in the field behind the hut and collecting potatoes in her apron. Not one by one like Mame, but a few together, without examining them. Mame examined every potato in the same way that she examined Gitale's clothes, closely checking each dress she took from the package that Stanislava had left. Gita did not remember these clothes, but the feel of them made her itchy even when she was no longer wearing them. Now she dressed in skirts and dresses with large collars. All the girls in the yard and on the street wore similar dresses. Mame loved to dress her and always examined her before going out to the street, to the market, or for a walk.

Her hair was no longer cut short. Gita proudly shook her head of new curly black hair, and that made Mame happy. For a while, Gita remembered how Stanislava used to comb Audra's yellow hair and braid it, but soon she began to forget.

"*Mein kind,* my child, you'll see how beautiful you will be," Mame told her. "You'll have curls and we'll put a ribbon in your hair." The Yiddish words were becoming more and more familiar and soon she began answering in Yiddish.

The apartment had two rooms connected by a wide door and a small kitchen. She was beginning to forget the smell of cooking in the big house on the farm. She retained only a vague memory of a pot of boiling water spilling on her. When that memory came up, she would caress the scar on her thigh and would feel the touch of egg yolk on her skin. At first, she would cry, then the memory became just a flash of thought.

In one room, the one with the window, there was a bed covered in a heavy brown bedspread that Tate and Mame opened at night, and there they slept. A brown table, with its clean white tablecloth and a decorative vase, stood in the center of the room. Gita especially loved the table because Mame agreed that she could draw there. But before she began, she always carefully placed the vase on the brown buffet, folded the tablecloth, and only then sat down on one of the four chairs around the table.

There were candlesticks on the buffet, and Mame would light candles in them just once a week. The buffet had three doors, one of which was almost always locked. Gita used to spy on Mame to see when she opened it. She wanted to find the things that Stanislava had put in the box. She especially hoped to find the cross with the figure of Jesus, so that once, just once, she could kiss him like Audra and Stanislava did and feel the pleasant warmth flowing inside her body. But there was no sign of Christ anywhere in the apartment. She endured a lot of beatings when she crossed herself like Audra and Stanislava. "We are Jews! You are Jewish!" Mame and Tate scolded her.

At night, before she went to bed, Gita would close her eyes tightly and ask for Good Jesus to help her. She no longer remembered where she had learned to make that nightly request, but it felt good. No one needed to know what she was doing.

She slept in the other room on the bed in the corner, where Tate sewed during the day at a black sewing machine made of iron. Multicolored spools of thread and a small pillow with needles rested on its wooden surface. All the clothes he sewed were placed in piles on the bed, and in the evening, before she went to bed, they were moved to the armchair that stood in the corner of the room. She was always obliged to wear shoes when she walked around the room, even when she got up at night, because pins and needles were on the floor everywhere. One time, a needle went into her foot. She burst into tears and was beaten by Tate because she hadn't listened to him about wearing shoes. She was once punished for remarking to Tate about his holding sewing pins in his mouth when working, while she was not allowed to play with the pins and stick them in the headless wooden mannequin kept in the room. Tate would dress this mannequin in dark suits, stick pins in them, and mark them with white chalk. In the first weeks, when the shadow of the mannequin lengthened at night, she would cry in fear, waiting for Grandma to come and hide with her in the barn. Then she got used to it and even talked to the mannequin in her room. She thought the mannequin looked like a scarecrow in a vegetable garden. When she went to bed, Gita lay curled up and listened to Mame and Tate's whispers. Sometimes they spoke quietly and pleasantly, and sometimes they shouted in anger. Almost always, Mame would silence Tate so he would not wake Gita. "Sha, sha, she's asleep." She learned to recognize her name among all the words spoken there quietly. And there were nights when she woke up hearing Tate shouting in his sleep, "Duvidl, *mein kind*!"

Gita's new home was located in an apartment building

in a neighborhood close to the city center. It was a four-story building built around a central courtyard that was covered with stone debris and tall grass for a long time. The mortar on the houses and in the stairwell was peeled off in many places, exposing red bricks, cement, and protruding steel bars. "It's because of the war," she heard the adults explain to guests who arrived there.

One day, a worker came with a cart and a horse, and for a whole day cleared the yard of debris so the children could play there.

Mame and Tate were busy all day. Tate sat by the rattling sewing machine and Mame cooked in the kitchen, cleaned, and helped Tate to mark the clothes and sew buttons and ribbons. She would stand for hours and iron the dark suits, skirts, and dresses people would bring to the apartment.

Gita found two corners in the apartment for herself. One was by the window facing the street, where she stood and examined the narrow spaces between the yards below and the narrow alleys between the houses. She loved to look at the sky, which was sometimes blue and sometimes gray and menacing. Looking out the window stirred a longing for open space that she could not explain to herself. Even the little birds that chirped and flew around the tree that almost reached the window became a source of longing. Sometimes, she took pieces of bread from her dress pocket, opened the window a little, laid crumbs on the ledge, and immediately closed it, smiling at the sight of the birds cheerfully pecking away.

In the other corner was a worn armchair made of dark red cloth. It had a high backrest and two dark armrests on each side. Two narrow slits in the cloth showed stripes of undefined color. "The upholstery needs to be replaced. Be careful not to tear what's there!" Mame would remind her, making her get up and then covering the seat with a piece of dark cloth. Gita would sit there holding a book or leaflet, eagerly examining each page, her lips moving to the rhythm of the letters she recognized.

When it was not raining, she was allowed to go down to the yard and play with the children who lived in the building. There were Sasha and Alexei, Isaiah and Fira, who spoke Yiddish with their parents, but spoke Lithuanian or Russian in the courtyard. There was also Zusia, who used to sit on a stone at the side, just watching the children without approaching them. When the boys played with their rag ball, the girls jumped rope at the corner of the yard. At first, Gita sat next to Zusia and they both watched the children playing enthusiastically. Gita's brown eyes were dreamy in the yard, just as they were when she stood by the window inside. Seeing her sitting like that, Mame sighed and said to Tate, "What does she see there, in her eyes and in her mind?"

One morning, Gita jumped resolutely from the fence she was sitting on, stood next to the girls who were jumping rope, pushed one of the girls turning the rope, and joined the group. And so, stubbornly, pushing, she secured her place; she always demanded to be first and did not give up her turn for anyone. Even when her legs tangled in the rope and she had to stop, she refused. She stamped her feet angrily and pushed the girl who was next in line, ignoring the girl's anger. After getting what she wanted, she left, sat down on the side, and was silent.

MAME PROMISED HER THAT AFTER THE SUMMER SHE WOULD start going to school and had chosen a top school where the language of instruction was Russian. In the meantime, she learned to combine syllables and letters into words in Lithuanian. She could already read complete sentences. Gita scribbled words in pencil on any piece of paper in the apartment: newspaper clippings or brown paper that was used for wrapping, almost everything. She was very upset when she discovered that only one letter was different in the names Rita and Gita.

Gita loved to go with Mame to the shopping district, even though these outings almost always ended in tears. Gita always demanded that Mame buy her a book. And while Mame was proud of her preschooler who could already read, she didn't like to spend the money. But she'd look through her bag for a few coins, argue with the seller, and eventually they'd hurry home with the book. They both knew Tate would be angry about the expenditure and would loudly shout: "Spoiled child! She only has books in her head! Does money grow on trees?" He would slam his hand so hard on the wooden surface of the sewing machine that the pins and threads would bounce.

Mame had several friends. There was Sonia, who had been with her in Russia. Every time they met, they reminisced in Yiddish about how hard and cold it had been there, about their need to hide and how worried they had been. And there was also Tate's cousin Asherke and his new wife, Ida.

From their conversations, Gita realized that Asherke had been with Tate in Kovno, in the ghetto. Tate then fled to Russia, while Asherke was sent to camps in Estonia. Tate's first wife and their son, David, were killed in the big *Aktion*. Every time they met, they would mention David, whose name Tate would scream at night. They sipped their tea, quickly ate the cake, and no one cared about Gita sitting on the armchair, browsing her booklets and taking in every word.

Once, because of something Tate said, she realized that it was because David had died that Tate was angry at her—even though she had never met him.

On the Jewish holidays, Tate went to the synagogue in a dark suit and a hat. He did not use his sewing machine and Mame prepared delicious dishes. Gita learned the difference between kneidlach, kreplach, and gefilte fish dipped in the spicy red horseradish sauce called chrein.

NOT EVERYONE APPRECIATED GITA'S INTELLIGENCE OR HER ability to read in both Lithuanian and Russian. Many of the children she knew were not nice to her about it at all.

One summer day, just before the start of the school year, she picked up a book, held it tightly under her arm, and went down to the yard between the houses, where the children were playing. She sat on a square stone and opened the book wide, so that anyone could see the cover with the Cyrillic letters.

She buried her face between the pages and started reading aloud, occasionally looking up to see whether the kids had noticed her. The older kids who were playing with the rag ball did. They approached her and stood around her in an intimidating ring.

Sergei, the largest and most powerful of the group, called out to her, "Hey you, intelligent Jew, who do you want to impress, huh?"

Her hands began to tremble. She rushed to close the book and looked for an escape route.

"Stinking Jew, show us the book!" said one of them, and he snatched it from her hands. "Look at that Communist Jew, see what she's reading!" He lifted the book up.

Thin little Gita waved her hands and tried to rise on her tiptoes to get her book back but withdrew because the group of children had begun to tear its pages and throw them around. She started running around the yard with the swinging ribbon on her head to snatch up the flying pages. She pursed her lips, not letting even a single tear appear on her face. It all lasted only a few minutes, but the experience was forever etched in her memory.

Zusia's mother heard the screams and ran to the yard. She shouted at the children and, holding Gita's hand, together they collected the pages left on the ground. "Anti-Semites," she murmured. "Come home. You must not go down to the yard with books."

When Tate saw her coming, he did not wait for an explanation. He forcibly took the book from Gita's clenched hands, threw it on the table, and Gita knew that now the beating would come. He made her lie on the couch, pulled up her dress, and hit her behind, blow after blow, shouting, "I'll show you how to behave! Only beatings will teach you not to embarrass us and not to get involved with bandits!" Gita put her face on her fists, pressed hard, and curled up like a hedgehog. After a few spanks, Mame pleaded, "Enough, stop, she understands."

The tension in the house after the incident in the yard eventually dissipated. Gita did not go downstairs, and instead began to prepare for school. Her parents got her a brown leather bag with three inner compartments and a leather cover with two buckles. On the back of the schoolbag, there were two leather straps that fit Gita's back. Tate used a thick needle to stitch one of the straps that was torn. He also got her proper outfits for school: brown dresses with pleats, white collars, and aprons in front.

Gita counted the days, repeatedly arranging the schoolbag with sheets of paper and pencils, taking out book after book and reading every word. She looked at the drawings in the booklets and scribbled numbers. Mame brought her an abacus with a wooden frame and colored beads. She passed beads from side to side and calculated how many she had added to the row and how many were missing. Gita could hardly wait to go to school. She would be a good student. They would notice that she already knew how to read and do arithmetic. She would not have to be home all day with Tate and Mame.

SCHOOLS IN VILNA WERE DIVIDED ACCORDING TO DISTRICTS, with each school assigned a number. The language of instruction was either Russian or Lithuanian. Gita went to a Russian-language school, number nine. Mame was very happy because she did not speak Lithuanian well. Only Tate was from Lithuania. Mame had grown up in Poland and then fled to Russia.

On the first day, Gita arrived at the school with Mame holding her hand. Mame put on her best clothes and held a small purse in her hand, while Gita was dressed in a school uniform: a dark dress with pleats and a white collar, ankle-high shoes, and white socks stretched to her knees. Her hair was brushed, and a large white ribbon hung on the right side of her head. When Mame whispered to Gita in Yiddish—"Be a good girl and look for friends. It's true you can read but you have to learn a whole lot of other things at school"—Gita pulled her hand away and answered her in Russian.

The school building stood at the corner of a main street. It was tall, a row of windows with open wooden shutters on each floor. Next to the building there was a large courtyard, free of stones and dirt. An iron fence covered with ivy enclosed the yard.

The first graders crowded into the yard and their parents were asked to leave. The principal stood there in a dark suit, and a beige shirt could be seen behind her collar. Her hair was pulled back, and she wore thick-framed glasses. The teachers stood beside her in a row, the men in suits and ties and the women in suits similar to that of the principal. Everyone was very serious. Their faces were turned to the principal as she greeted the children. They were asked to stand at attention as the red flag with the hammer and sickle emblazoned on it fluttered on the side. Then they read out the names and pointed where each child should go and announced who their teacher was.

Gita rose on her tiptoes. Taller children stood around her. She turned her head left and right and tried to identify a familiar face among the students. She examined the line of teachers and saw a teacher with braided blond hair gathered at the nape of her neck. I wish for her to be my teacher, she begged in her heart. The number of children in the plaza decreased. Maybe they won't call me? Her hands were clenched, but then she heard her name, Gita Ruhin. Group six. The teacher was not the one she had hoped for. Her teacher's name was Marina Sreisky and her hair was short and brown.

The children sat on wooden chairs in front of the teacher's desk, behind which hung a blackboard with words and letters written on it. Gita began to read quietly. A tall girl sitting next to her, with blond hair and blue eyes, looked at her and whispered, "Shhh." Next to the board was a picture of Stalin. His image was not unfamiliar to her. She even liked him, though older men usually scared her. She saw his picture in many places, even in the newspapers, where she diligently read the printed words slowly and understood that he was good to everyone. He was their savior. She also heard Tate and Mame talk about him many times. The adults claimed that without Stalin, the Red Army, and the Russians, there would have been no one to save them. Sometimes they said it out loud.

The teacher taught them rules of conduct. They learned to raise a hand and ask for permission to speak and to stand upright at their table as the teacher entered the classroom.

"When are we going to read?" Gita whispered.

"Shhh!" She was silenced again by blond Julia sitting next to her. The teacher turned an angry look at them. "Hands up!" she commanded, and all the children raised their hands.

In the days that followed, Gita was moved next to Anna. Like Gita, Anna could read, and they both were quick to raise their hands and answer the teacher's questions accurately. After each correct answer, Gita turned her head to the rest of the students with a smile of victory on her lips. In her notebooks, she wrote everything meticulously. She and Anna would compare the text in their notebooks. They both looked at the other children and smiled every time one of them answered incorrectly or had difficulty reading the text.

The school was the safest place for Gita. She absorbed the Russian language taught by the teachers and it became the language she spoke. She read and wrote quickly and without errors. Everything interested her. At every question the teacher asked, she swung her hand up straight and high as required, and the teacher, who also wanted to hear the answers of other children, caught Gita's disappointed look. She already knew the forward movement of her chin, her lips twitching and expressing insult for being left out, her answer ignored.

She was an outstanding student, and the Russian school indeed appreciated students like her. At the awards ceremony, she was invited to the stage, and the principal shook her hand. In the math competitions between classes and between schools, she was always among the finalists.

Toward the end of her second school year, the parents of all the students were invited to a meeting with the teacher. At the end of the school day, Gita approached her teacher and announced that her mother would not be able to come because she was ill.

"So maybe Dad can come?" asked the teacher.

"He's sick too," Gita replied.

"Too bad, I want them to hear good things about you. Maybe they can come another day."

"I don't think so," Gita tersely replied.

"We'll see what we can do." The teacher was trying to comfort her, but Gita's evasive eyes made Mrs. Sreisky suspicious.

Gita did not want Mame to come to school because she was ashamed of Mame's appearance and speech. And Tate, who did not really like the Communist Party and the

Soviets, would probably not want to come. How good it was for her friend Anna that her father was a communist and a high-ranking Russian official and could come to his daughter's school.

She thought of all the excuses she could come up with just so her mame would not come and talk to Mrs. Sreisky. In the evening, Mame looked at the student's diary that was lying on the table and saw the invitation to the parents. "What's this?" she asked, and Gita immediately blurted, "It's been canceled. You don't have to go."

"Why?" asked Mame.

"Because the teacher is sick and won't be able to meet the parents of our class."

Mame was disappointed. She knew she would only hear good things about her daughter at school and longed for some compliments and kind words. She checked with one of the Jewish mothers whose daughter was studying with Gita and learned that the teacher was not ill and that the meetings would take place as specified in the invitation. Mame did not understand Gita's motives and assumed that she had simply made a mistake.

When Mame returned from the meeting with the teacher, her eyes shone. She smiled at Gita and told her and Tate, who sat quietly and even smiled a little, "The teacher was so nice and welcoming, and what good things she said about our Gita. She excels in all classes, and all her grades are five out of five."

At the end of the second school year, Gita was elected top of her class.

●

ANNA LIVED NOT FAR FROM GITA. YIDDISH WAS SOMETIMES spoken at her home too. Her mame had a blue number tattooed on her wrist, a long number that Gita had already seen on people's arms. When they saw her looking at the number on their arm, they would pull their sleeve down and reflexively rub it. One neighbor even put an adhesive band on her arm to cover the blue number.

Gita loved visiting Anna. She had a little brother named Isaac, and her father was a communist and worked outside the house. Gita thought it was good to have a father who wasn't home—that way no one would shout or get angry. The father was a high-ranking official in one of the government ministries and also knew Russian, and in Anna's house there were books in Russian. Gita envied her for that.

Mame did not like the association between Gita and Anna, especially not Gita's frequent visits to their home. One winter day after school, Gita asked Anna if she could come visit. "My parents are not home," Gita said. "They had to go somewhere." Anna welcomed the idea and the two friends walked to Anna's home.

"Does your mom know you're here?" asked Anna's mother.

"Yes," Gita replied briefly, and hurried to play with Isaac.

"Come and eat with us," suggested Anna's mother.

Gita rested her head on her hands and watched the

thick soup with the large potatoes being poured into the bowls. She thought of Mame, who must already have served Tate the food because he would soon go and rest. He would not even notice that Gita had not yet returned. He had yelled at her the day before when she returned from school. She had run to the window to watch snowflakes drifting slowly in the air and did not notice that her mame was calling her to the table. "Come to the table before I take off my belt and let you taste it!" Tate shouted at her. Let them both be there alone, she thought to herself. They are not happy that I am with them anyway.

"Eat," Anna's mother told her. Anna had already finished eating and suggested that Gita come and look at the new booklets she had received. She finished the hot soup and went to sit with Anna on the couch and peruse the booklets. Two hours later, she had completely forgotten about her home. "When is your mother coming to pick you up?" Anna's mother asked in a troubled voice. "They went far," Gita said. "Maybe I should just stay here?"

Anna's mother was about to answer when they heard nervous knocks on the door. She ran to open the door. Mame stormed into the room, saw Gita, and slapped her in the face. "Bad girl, get home right away!" Then she shouted at Anna's mother in Yiddish, "Is that how you behave? Didn't you know we'd be worried sick about her? What is she, a street girl?" She dragged Gita by force. Anna's family members watched with their mouths agape.

"No one is taking your girl," Anna's mother said, and

then turned to Gita. "Never lie to me again, you hear? I will not let Anna be your friend! A girl who lies will not come into our house!"

Gita buried her eyes in the floor. "Just wait and see what Tate will do to you," Mame said as she dragged her out of Anna's apartment. Gita said nothing.

"Just tell us what you want from us!" Tate shouted, as he beat her later. "Didn't we suffer enough from the Lithuanians, the Nazis, and the war? You have to punish us too?" He grabbed her arm, led her into the room, and locked the door. "You will go to bed without supper."

In the summer, Gita returned to play with Zusia, the girl from upstairs who was supposed to start first grade. Gita volunteered to be her teacher as they played "school." She held a small stick in her hand and pointed to an imaginary wall behind her.

In the days when she did not play with Zusia, she read. Almost every day she went to a library two blocks away and exchanged books. The librarian admired the girl who finished reading books so quickly. The amiable, blue-eyed library manager was always nice to her as well.

One summer day, Gita persuaded Zusia to go for a walk. She led Zusia to the house where Anna had lived. Mame had informed her that Anna and her family were gone, and that Anna's nice father had been taken away in the middle of the night, but Gita didn't believe her. Her nice father could not have been taken to Siberia, that place adults only whispered about. How could Anna not have told her where they were? And what about cute little Isaac and their kind mother?

She went upstairs to Anna's apartment, but a stranger opened the door. Gita took Zusia's hand, and they hurried back to their building. When they returned to the yard, Mame came toward them. She took Gita in one hand and Zusia in the other and led them home fiercely. "Who allowed you to go for a walk?"

Zusia immediately burst into tears, while Gita pursed her lips tightly and tried to free herself from Mame's grip.

"Just wait, and see what punishment you get," Mame hissed.

At home, Gita explained to Mame that she had gone to see if Anna was home. Maybe all the stories about her father were not true at all.

"Stupid girl," Mame growled, "those are not stories. We've told you several times not to go there. They shouldn't know that we had any contact with them. Stay home and don't go down to the yard, and woe if you tell anyone what you did."

ONCE EVERY FEW MONTHS, MAME WOULD BRING HOME A package of brown cardboard tied with strong wires. The packages came from America, Mame said. She opened the four-winged lid with scissors; the package emitted a strange odor. Mame pulled out garment after garment, examined each one individually like the vegetables she bought at the market. She made one pile of the clothes that impressed her and a second pile of clothes that she did not like at all. There were clothes of different fabrics and assorted sizes. Transparent blouses made of soft and unfamiliar fabrics, colorful pleated skirts, headscarves in red, pink, and bright blue. "Who will wear them here?" Mame would say.

The packages often included boxes with milk powder, egg powder, chocolate with a special flavor, and a box of chicory. These sparked great joy. Mame tried to sell the rejected clothes clandestinely to neighbors in exchange for a few rubles. Tate offered the ties to his clients.

At first, Gita wanted to know who had sent the packages, but she only received short answers. "A family living in America," Mame said, and never uttered the name "Goldberg." Eventually, the packages stopped coming when the Iron Curtain closed. "Someone up there stopped them."

GITA WAS GLAD WHEN SUMMER VACATION WAS OVER. SHE preferred the order and schedule of school. And she had a passion for studying, especially geography. She loved to look at the map spread on the wall in front of the blackboard. Names of countries and major cities that she knew from the books she had read appeared on the map. There was Moscow and Leningrad, which the Nazis, damn them, put under siege, but the heroic Red Army managed to defeat them. The Red Army, led by Stalin, liberated Lithuania and Vilna and also saved the Jews who had fled to Russia.

Her eyes often wandered over the names of the cities to which she felt connected—such as Bialystok in Poland, where Mame was from. She studied the blue areas that marked the seas and found it curious that one blue-painted sea was called the "Black Sea." Her eyes once came across an area called Siberia, which was very far from Vilna. She was so frightened that she immediately stopped looking.

In math lessons, the teacher called her to the board, and she felt like a magician solving the formulas he scribbled there. But more than any of the lessons, she loved literature. She read and reread the books the teacher recommended, and recited verses of poetry again and again.

Anna never returned to school. Instead, Gita made friends with Ilonka and other students. Mame questioned her about her friends, and Gita knew she wanted to know which of her classmates were Jewish. At first, it was hard for her to recognize them, but over time she learned to discern who was Jewish. She met some of the Jews when she went to synagogue. That year was the first time Mame took her there. Every Jew went there on Jewish holidays.

In the synagogue, Gita crossed herself as she sometimes did inadvertently when passing a church on the street or when she was scared. This time Mame pulled her hand forcibly and looked anxiously around her. "I'm going home with you right away," she scolded her. Gita tried to free her hand from Mame's grip. Other mothers looked at her and at Mame angrily. Inside the synagogue they sat in the part reserved only for women.

Gita noticed some women looking at her all the time. An hour later, Mame whispered something in her friend Ida's ear, took Gita's hand, and they left the synagogue. Gita actually wanted to go home, but not as a punishment. They were both silent. When they arrived at the apartment, Mame entered the kitchen, hid her face in a plaid cloth, and wiped her nose silently. A few minutes later, Gita saw her sitting on the stool, crying and making noises as if she were suffocating. Gita was startled, ran away, curled up in her armchair, and clutched a book, but did not read it.

Mame never took Gita to synagogue again.

IN THE SPRING, A LARGE GROUP OF JEWS TRAVELED TO the Ponary Forest. Mame took Gita with her, and there were also other children on the train. After a few stops, they could no longer see the houses of Vilna. With the coming of spring, new leaves sprouted on the trees they viewed from the windows. The group got off at a small station and people whispered to each other: "They were murdered here." The parents kept the children close to them. Mame held Gita's hand.

Without anyone asking or directing, people began to spread out, and from every corner there were cries: "Mame," "Tate," "Moishele," and other names. Gita's Mame stood with a few other women at the entrance to a pit with pink edges and steps leading to the bottom.

"What is this?" Gita asked.

"Be quiet now," Mame silenced her, took out a handkerchief, and began to weep.

Ilonka, her parents, and two other friends from school were also there, but they did not approach one another, just exchanged glances and fell silent. Eventually everyone gathered in a forest clearing. In the center of the clearing, a sign was mounted on a pile of stones. The letters on the sign were written from right to left and looked nothing like Russian or Lithuanian.

"That's how you write in Yiddish," Mame explained to her.

"What is written here?" Gita asked.

"*Gedenk unzere brider und schwester.*" Mame explained: "A memorial for our brothers and sisters."

Men who were not wearing their hats now placed them on their heads, and the sound of prayer was heard in the woods.

The group walked again in silence to the train station. Raspberry and currant bushes lined the sides of the road. Children who tried to bend over to pick their favorite fruit, as they were accustomed to doing when they went for walks in the forests around the city, were cautioned by their parents. "Not here," they were told. "Not here."

"It was sad there," Gita said softly to Ilonka. "Did you see everyone crying?"

"Of course they were crying. If people had murdered your mother and father and shot your brothers and sisters because they were Jews, wouldn't you have cried?"

A few days later, Gita saw Ilonka talking to two of her friends. As she approached, she heard Ilonka say to them, "Her father was a doctor and not a tailor." Had Ilonka not covered her mouth with her hand when she noticed her, Gita would not have suspected that they were talking about her. But Ilonka's panic and the surprised eyes of her friends puzzled Gita. What does that mean, he was a doctor and not a tailor? Tate? What had Ilonka's mother told her? But she chose not to ask, and just wrote the questions in a private notebook she kept in a hiding place. The notebook was like a diary she had read about in a book. Gita recorded all her questions and feelings in the notebook. She now felt there was a secret to be revealed.

THE CUSTOM OF CELEBRATING BIRTHDAYS MADE GITA uncomfortable, especially the one Ilonka's parents held in their home. Unlike Gita's house, Ilonka's had three rooms and an indoor toilet and bath. On her birthday, her mother made her a cake and there were other sweets. They played games and had a wonderful time. When the party was over and it was time to go home, Gita thought about her room, with Tate at his sewing machine and Mame in the kitchen, and she did not want to return.

Instead of politely thanking Ilonka and leaving like the other girls, Gita snarled at Ilonka, "You shouldn't be showing off with your house and your birthday party. It was not at all as beautiful as you think."

Ilonka looked at her in astonishment. "If you don't like me, then don't come over anymore. Just to let you know, I know things about you that you do not know!"

"How was it?" Mame asked Gita as she stormed into the house. "Why are you sad? Did something happen?"

"When's my birthday? You never celebrate my birthday. I don't even know the date of my birthday!" Gita shot at her.

In the morning, Mame approached her and said, "You were born on the twentieth of November, 1943."

Gita examined her mother's face. Something in the hesitant way she spoke made her uncomfortable. "I was born then?"

"Yes," Mame replied.

"So why have you never told me that before?

Mame sat down heavily on the stool, wiped sweat from her forehead, and sighed. "How horrid you can be to me," she whispered.

Gita softened. Something in Mame's tired and despairing look touched her heart, and she relented. At school, she would tell Ilonka that because her birthday had long since passed, she would not be celebrating this year. When she arrived in class, she saw Ilonka at the center of a group of girls. As she passed them, she again heard Ilonka say, "Her father was once a doctor and today he's a tailor." Now she knew for sure that they were gossiping about her, but why was Ilonka telling this stupid story again? How could Tate be a doctor? After all, he had always been a tailor. When the girls noticed Gita, they fell silent. Gita decided to ignore them. She set her chin forward and walked to the classroom.

In the months remaining until the end of the school year, she distanced herself from her friends, and books were her only companions. She finished this school year with honors too.

DURING THE SUMMER VACATION, SHE TRAVELED WITH Mame and a group of Jews to Kovno. They went to visit the site of the ghetto and place a monument there. When Mame quietly told Tate about the plan in the kitchen the evening before, Gita heard him raise his voice. "I'm not going back to that place. What do I need to see there? Do I really need to revisit the place where they took David? To recite *kaddish* for the boy they murdered? I will not return to that place."

Mame quieted him down. "Be calm so the girl doesn't hear."

"If you take her to Kovno with the whole group, she might hear the stories about . . ."

"Shhh! Be quiet!" Mame shouted at him. Then she got up, left the kitchen, and went to check on Gita, who hurriedly stuck her head in a book. Gita wrote that day in her notebook: "I know they're hiding a secret from me. And I know Tate doesn't like me, as though it's my fault he doesn't have his Duvidl. But what's their secret? One thing I understand: Duvidl was not Mame's child. Only Tate misses him.

But I don't understand what it has to do with what Ilonka says, that once he was a doctor and now he's a tailor. I hope Mame takes me to Kovno without him. Maybe I'll ask her there."

The group that boarded the train also included Ilonka and her parents. Her mother was wearing an elegant suit and a fashionable hat. She heard two women from the group whisper, "Well, is that how people come dressed for a memorial in the ghetto?" Now Gita cheered up. Ilonka's mother was also being talked about behind her back. Gita felt less alone, and less uncomfortable about approaching Ilonka, who smiled at Gita as if they had not been upset with each other for several weeks.

In Kovno, a group of people was waiting for them. "These are Jews living in Kovno," Mame explained to Gita. The group began to walk toward the bridge. The women and men marched heavily, most of them bowing their heads, while the children ran to and fro, ignoring the shouts of their parents trying to silence them.

Suddenly Ilonka's mother began to cry and screamed in Yiddish, "Mommy, Mame, where are you? I cannot walk alone!" Her cries provoked shouting and weeping among the marchers. Ilonka ran to her mother, but she sat down on the sidewalk and refused to move. Gita watched the woman who had previously been mocked for her fancy dress sitting pale in her suit on the stones. Ilonka waved the hat that she had removed from her mom's head to give her some air. The group found it difficult to move forward. Some people announced that they didn't have the strength to go to that place. But Mame was among those marching forward. She dragged Gita along and said, "We have to be strong! We have to respect the people who died here. We are alive. We have to respect those who didn't make it."

"Maybe Tate didn't want to come because he didn't want to experience what happened to Ilonka's mother?" Gita asked.

"Maybe," Mame replied, and kept walking.

Gita did not want to leave Ilonka. She did not understand why the people were crying and yet insisted on going to a place they called the ghetto. She understood that the Nazis had killed many Jews in this place, but why was this relevant to her? After all, the Red Army had saved them. In the marching group, there were two women she had met before; she was sure of it, but she did not know where. They were with a boy of about thirteen with blue eyes, who walked quietly beside them. Gita was bothered by their presence because they were staring at her. They smiled at her as she looked at them but did not say a word. Suddenly Mame saw the looks Gita exchanged with the two. She took her hand and pulled her away. "Don't you go anywhere, do you hear?" she warned. And again, Gita shuffled behind Mame while her eyes searched for something new to observe.

Gita saw a Lithuanian who spat toward them as he passed and said, "They all should have been killed then." She was frightened and held Mame's hand tightly. Her eyes searched for others who might have heard the Lithuanian curse them and noticed that one of the two women who had been watching her was now pointing to a ruined structure standing near the plaza. "That's where Jonah's hospital was," she said. The second woman glanced at Gita and said, "Let's get out of here."

On the train ride home, no one said a word. People kept fanning Ilonka's mother with her hat and offering her water. Ilonka swung her legs and kept her eyes glued to the floor of the moving train.

MAME DID NOT TAKE HER ONLY TO SAD PLACES THAT summer. She also took her to one of the lakes in the Tarkai area. They slept in a hut they rented for a few days from a Lithuanian. Asherke and Ida also came with them. The adults played cards, and Gita sat with the books she had brought with her and read. There were other children there, but she had no desire to meet them. When Mame handed her a swimsuit with an open back, she covered it with a shirt so that no one could see the scars that Tate's beatings had left. But Ida managed to see. She asked Mame quietly, "What is that?" And Mame hurried to answer, "It's from the farm. They used to beat her there." Mame motioned to Gita to keep quiet, and Gita glared back at Mame with a piercing look.

When she went swimming, she dunked her head and counted how long she could stay underwater. Maybe if I stop breathing, I'll just stop being, she thought. Then Mame would not have to lie because of me, and Tate would be free of me. But when she ran out of air, she pulled her head from the water, took a deep breath, and looked for Mame. Is she watching me? Does she worry about me?

In early March they learned that Stalin was very ill. Mame said he would not survive. And indeed, the news from Moscow came a few days later: "Stalin the hero, Father of Nations, is dead!" The students received the news in the morning at school. The principal stood before them and announced his death in a broken voice and then burst into tears. The teachers who stood in a line around her also cried. They took handkerchiefs from their pockets and wiped their tears. Sobs were heard from the children's rows. A few minutes of rising noise and cries of grief passed and then the principal regained her composure and shouted for everyone to return to the ranks, respect the difficult hour, and be as strong as their leader would expect of them. Heavy mourning prevailed everywhere. Black ribbons were placed on Stalin's pictures. The teachers in the classrooms talked about the leader, the hero of World War II who had saved them from the cruel Nazi occupier, the peace-seeking man who advanced industry and brought honor to the toiling people. When Gita got home that day, she asked Mame to hang a picture of Stalin, and she looked for a piece of black cloth in Tate's sewing room to put on it.

She very much hoped that Tate would not object and that they would understand that she was very sad that day and wanted them to be sad, too, because lately she had heard them and their acquaintances whispering a lot about the trial of Jewish doctors in Moscow. She thought how good it would be if they were not Jews. She would do anything not to be Jewish. To be Jewish was to be different, and she did not even know why.

And indeed, as she had guessed, a quarrel broke out. Mame agreed to hang Stalin's picture, but Tate quietly announced, "In my house, it is out of the question." Gita gave up. Mourning for Stalin died down, and a few days later, the newspaper and radio announced that the doctors had been released. Asherke and Ida said that things would be easier now.

WITH STALIN'S DEATH AND THE RELEASE OF THE DOCTORS, there was less talk of another disaster awaiting the Jews. At school, a picture of Stalin was replaced by the Soviet flag. The counselors in the Communist youth movement continued to glorify the Communist Party and Socialist theory. Gita and her friends would go to youth movement activities dressed in uniforms and wearing a red tie around their necks. She loved going to these activities, taking trips and engaging in discussions with the counselors, and she savored the opportunity to be out of the house.

Tate became ill. For many days, he lay in bed and did not get up to mend clothes, and customers stopped coming. He stared at the high ceiling and sighed. At night, he coughed and shouted Duvidl's name even louder.

"He is not young anymore," Mame whispered to her friend Sonia. "He no longer has any strength. He's lost patience with life. I knew why I wanted a girl. What will happen to me? I'm still young. She at least gives me the opportunity to be a mother and not just live with a sick man." Sonia nodded in agreement.

When Tate felt better, he sat down at the sewing machine, completed suit alterations, and sewed dresses from fabrics that acquaintances, who remembered him from his better days, would bring him.

AS SHE GREW OLDER, GITA FELT TATE'S EVASIVE LOOKS more and more, and Mame's attempts to appease her with clothes and praise for her academic successes. But what bothered her most of all were the many prohibitions that Mame imposed on her, the incessant interrogations about whom she had met and what she had heard in the homes of her friends. All of these reinforced her suspicion that a great secret shrouded their home.

In her imagination, she saw a wooden box full of secrets. There must be a box like that hidden somewhere in the house. If she opened it, the whispers between Tate and Mame would become clearer. Mame's bewildered looks would disappear and her conversations with Sonia, Asherke, and Ida would no longer leave her feeling that they were somehow conspiring against her. Gita would discover what was behind the story of the doctor who was now a tailor.

When she was alone at home, she searched for the mysterious box. She opened every drawer and climbed up to the high shelves in the kitchen. But she found no such box.

In recent months, she began feeling that what seemed to be chance encounters with people were not accidental at all. People lingered beside her as if trying to tell her something and then hurriedly disappeared. Particularly disturbing was a slender man with blue eyes who watched her from behind the school fence. She noticed him several times and finally approached him. He continued to look at her and even smile. The man hesitantly raised his hand a little, as if waving hello to her and then regretting it. It's the smile of a good man, she thought. She was sure he was seeking to make contact. His gaze lingered on her face again, and she had no doubt that he was addressing her personally, that he knew her.

She decided to tell Mame about the man with the blue eyes. She hurried up the stairs in the dim stairwell and entered quietly so that Tate, who was sitting next to the sewing machine, would not notice her. She was tired of his growling, of his anger.

The sewing machine was rattling, and she went into the kitchen where Mame was standing. The smell of the large potatoes frying vied with the aroma of the fried onions. Mame wiped her hands on the stained apron.

"Hmm," she murmured when she noticed her. "How was school?"

"Good," Gita replied, and sat on the wooden chair.

She propped her head on one hand and with the other hand played with the breadcrumbs on the table.

"Mame," she said hesitantly, "there's a man who has come to school several times already. He stands by the fence and looks at me."

Mame stopped her work and gazed at Gita with wide eyes. Gita saw the anxiety in her face.

"What man?" Mame asked.

"He's thin, tall, and has blue eyes."

"Did he talk to you?"

"No, he just smiles at me and walks away."

"You're just imagining it," Mame said.

"I don't think so! Today he spoke to Ilonka. Ilonka knows him."

"Nonsense." Mame's voice trembled. "Nonsense."

"You probably know him," Gita tried again.

"I told you it's nonsense! You keep putting nonsense in your head all the time," Mame said. She was silent for a few minutes and then asked, "Is it the man who was at Ilonka's birthday? The one whose daughter is Ilonka's friend?"

Gita was surprised that her mother suddenly brought up Ilonka's birthday. What's the connection? she wondered. Gita grew angry. She began to feel that the lump in her chest was slowly expanding and whispering to her: something is wrong here, they are lying.

"Was Tate once a doctor?" she asked.

Mame stood motionless, planted like a tree in the

middle of the kitchen. There was a scary silence. Then came Mame's strangled voice: "Where did you hear such stories?"

"Ilonka told me she heard her parents talking about this."

"They don't know what they are talking about," Mame continued angrily. "They're jealous that you're such a good student! Don't ask Ilonka about that man you saw! I've warned you so many times not to talk to strangers."

Gita felt she was going to burst into tears. Her chest was about to explode. Mame must not see. She got up in a rush and ran to the bathroom.

TATE FELL ILL AGAIN.

Mame summoned Gita: "Take the note the doctor left and go to the pharmacy to get medicine for Tate. Take a coat, the sun is misleading; it's very cold outside." Gita was happy for the opportunity to leave the house.

She chose to skip the pharmacy at the end of the street, where they usually bought medicine. If I go to the pharmacy a few blocks from here, she thought, I can stay out longer. I'll tell Mame that our pharmacy didn't have the medicine we needed.

The distant pharmacy had caught her attention. Each time they walked in that area, it seemed to her that Mame avoided getting close to it. Gita entered confidently. When she opened the door, the bell rang. There were rows of shelves with brown glass jars and white stickers on them.

She approached a white wooden table covered with green glass. A gray-haired pharmacist in a white gown emerged from the back room with a smile on his face.

When he saw her, he narrowed his eyes, adjusted his glasses to the bridge of his nose, and bent down slightly to focus his gaze on her. Gita felt embarrassed and took a step back.

Suddenly the pharmacist straightened up and said with a smile, "You must be Dr. Jonah Freidman's daughter. Such likeness!" he gushed.

Gita's face turned pale. She tried to plant her feet firmly on the floor so that the tremor she felt would not knock her down. She felt drums pounding in her chest. She had heard the name Jonah Freidman whispered more than once.

And now it all made sense: Tate is not my father! And I am not their daughter!

"What happened?" the smiling pharmacist asked. "Are you ill? I remember your father well. What a doctor, what a wonderful person he was."

"No, no, everything's fine," she replied with pursed lips.

The pharmacist stopped talking. He was quite sure she was Jonah Freidman's daughter, but who could tell, the whole world had turned upside down. Better not to interfere. He prepared the prescription, put the medicine in a brown bag, and handed it to Gita. "Good day to you," he said.

Gita's palm locked on to the brown bag with the medicine, and she started running away from the pharmacy.

Now I know, now I know, she said to herself over and over again. The lump in her throat threatened to suffocate her. The pharmacist knows the truth. I'm the doctor's daughter.

She sat down on a bench on the sidewalk and coughed to loosen the lump in her throat. Her tears flowed. Passersby gazed at the girl sitting on the bench and weeping, her legs shaking and a bag of medicine in her hand. But still, no one stopped.

I'm not their daughter! I'm not their daughter! The words drilled into her head. Tate hates me because I'm not his daughter. Maybe they kidnapped me. She relaxed her grip on the medicine bag and began to walk toward Ilonka's house, determined not to return home until she discovered the truth.

Ilonka's mother opened the door and was startled by what she saw. "What happened? Why are you crying? What's up?" Gita's swollen eyes and the bag of medicine in her hand left no room for doubt that something bad had happened.

"Come in," Ilonka's mother said. "Tell me what's going on."

Gita let herself be led to a chair in the center of the room and then, in simple words, said, "The man at the pharmacy said I was Dr. Jonah Freidman's daughter and that I looked very much like him. Jonah is my father!"

Ilonka's mother stifled a cry and raised her palm to her mouth. "Gita," she said a few seconds later, "you need to go home."

"I want to know the truth!" Gita shouted.

Ilonka's mother gently stroked her and asked what she had in her hands.

"Medications for Tate."

"Go home and give Tate the medicine. He's sick. I promise to talk to you in a few days. In the meantime, don't upset Mame and Tate. They are not well."

Through her tears, Gita saw Ilonka's father enter the house. Ilonka's mother put her finger on her lips, hinting at him to be silent. Without another word, she wrapped Gita's shoulders in a scarf, picked up her coat, and went out with her toward Tate and Mame's house. Gita walked beside her in silence and her legs were heavy.

"Gitale, listen to me," said Ilonka's mother, placing a warm hand on her shoulder, "I can't go home with you. I cannot interfere in the affairs of another family. I suggest you go up and tell them what happened at the pharmacy."

Mame was already waiting at the stairwell door, about to head out to look for Gita. As soon as Gita appeared, she started shouting, "Where have you been? How long does it take to buy medicine? Where did you go? I didn't know what happened to you!" Her face flushed and she snatched the bag from Gita's hands. "You're always looking for trouble. We'll have to punish you again!"

Gita did not look at Mame's face. Her lips became a thin slit, and she started running up the stairs without saying a word and without explaining anything. Mame climbed after her and arrived, panting, at the apartment.

Gita sat down in the kitchen, her eyes staring and her legs bouncing. "What happened?" Mame asked.

Suddenly Gita jumped to her feet and stood tall, with clenched fists. Pressing her chin close to Mame's face, she said, "I know you're not my mother and Tate is not my father. You took me from the father I had, who was a doctor. You lied to me all the time. I know the truth. I don't want to stay with you even one more day!"

Mame let out a cry and collapsed on the stool. Her face was red and covered with sweat. "Oy! Oy!" she yelled. Tate dragged himself to the kitchen. "Liars!" Gita hissed, and did not move. The slap was not long in coming. "No slap will hide the truth," Gita continued, and Mame burst into tears.

Long minutes passed before Mame could tell Tate what she had just heard from Gita.

"Get out of here," Tate shouted. "Go!"

"I will go only after you tell me who my father and mother were. Who is Jonah Freidman? Where did you take me from? I want my real father and mother. You are not my parents!"

"Who told you that?" Mame asked in a pleading voice.

"The pharmacist where I bought the medications. He told me that my father is Dr. Jonah Freidman. Ilonka and her mother also know that."

Tate glared at Mame and left the kitchen.

"It's not like that, my child. You're our girl because we took you in after the war. Both your mother and your father were killed in the ghetto in the war. We took you in. We didn't want you to suffer. We thought you'd be fine if you felt you had a mother and father. What good would it be for you to know that your father and mother were killed in the war, or that the wretched Nazis murdered them? Many families took Jewish children whose parents were murdered. We wanted you to be happy, not to be afraid, and not to grow up as an orphan."

Gita's rigid posture and clenched fists loosened a bit. Tears welled up in her brown eyes.

"I want my mother and father," she whimpered. "I want to know who they were. I don't want you. I don't want Tate, who only knows how to get angry and beat me. I had a feeling you weren't my parents. Real mothers and fathers don't hit and punish like you do."

Nothing could stop the tears flowing in the kitchen. That night, Mame's world crashed, and Gita's world began to be woven anew.

Gita did not go to school the next day. Mame went out in the morning and came back with Ida. When Ida entered the apartment, she rushed to Gita and tried to hug her, but Gita pushed her away.

"You lied to me too," she cried.

"Come on, Gitale, let's sit and talk," Ida said softly. "It's not so simple. Mame loves you and she wants only the best for you. And so does Tate."

"They lied to me the whole time. Maybe they kidnapped me from my father, like Gypsies? If they want what's good for me, then why does Tate keep hitting me? There's just one child he constantly thinks about, and that's Duvidl. It's not me he loves!"

"I came with Mame now to tell you everything that happened. If you listen to us, maybe something good will come from it in the end."

Gita sulked silently in her corner, resisting the efforts of the two women to communicate with her. The sudden movement of Mame's chair made Gita look up. She saw Mame get up and walk toward the buffet. She pulled out a small key from under a miniature doll, went to the sideboard, and opened a narrow drawer that Gita had never noticed. Mame pulled out a brown, crumpled envelope. "Here," she said. "Come see."

Despite her curiosity, Gita turned her head. "I don't want anything from you!"

Ida ignored her and said to Mame, "Show me what's in the envelope." Mame pulled pictures and papers out of the envelope.

"Do you want to see?" Ida asked Gita. "You were born in the Kovno ghetto, and this was your father." She walked over to Gita and handed her a small picture showing a tall man with black hair, wearing a white robe and holding a medical device in his hands. "Your father was a doctor in the ghetto. The accursed Germans murdered him when the ghetto was burned down. And here's a picture of your mother. Here they are both together. She was murdered, along with your father."

Gita's chin trembled. Ida asked Mame, "Where are these pictures from?"

"From the Gentile."

"Which Gentile?" Gita asked, and a few more pictures were placed in front of her. One picture showed a woman with blond hair braided around her head and two young girls, one on each side of the woman. The older one was also blond, but the younger, brown-eyed girl had almost no hair.

"Who is she?" cried Gita. The woman in the picture reminded her of someone she had once seen. The sound of her voice echoed in her head: "I know her."

"This woman received you from your father after he smuggled you out of the ghetto so that the Germans wouldn't catch you. Your father placed you in her care."

Gita cried softly. The two women also shed tears.

Gita closed her eyes. A barrage of images raced through her mind: a tiny pig's wet nose rubbing her arms on a haystack; a bumpy train ride alongside the woman and the girl; an old woman in a headscarf hugging her; a chilly grain barn; a girl teaching her to read; someone cutting her hair; Tate hitting her; the man with the blue eyes; the blue-eyed woman at the library; the woman who talked to her during the trip to Kovno for the ceremony.

"Is the man who watched me at the school from my family? And what about the woman who runs the library?" The two women opened their mouths. Mame sought help in Ida's eyes, and the latter decided to take the reins. She could no longer bear the girl's misery. Mame shrugged in her chair and was silent, and Ida told her, "Yes, both are from your father's family."

"I don't want to stay here," Gita declared. "I want to go to my father's family!"

"We will connect you with your uncle, Mr. Goldberg, and with your aunt, Mrs. Dinner, from the library," Ida said. "They can tell you the whole story about your father and mother. But you cannot run away from home like that. We'll consider what to do."

"Gitale," Mame murmured, holding out her hand to caress Gita, but Gita turned her head away and returned to the armchair in the corner with her father's picture in her hands.

The next day, when school was over, Gita went straight to the library. She climbed the stairs to the second floor, to the office where Leike Dinner was sitting. Leike raised her head and smiled at her, and her blue eyes lit up.

"Mrs. Dinner," Gita whispered, "I know that you're a cousin of Jonah Freidman. And I know that Jonah Freidman is my real father."

Leike looked at her in astonishment. "How do you know? Who told you?" she asked. "Do your mom and dad know that you know?"

"Yes." Gita stared with her large, wide-open eyes into Leike's face. "I have known for a long time that they are not my parents. You have to tell me everything!"

"I'll tell you everything, but not now and not here. Come to my house with your mother and then we'll talk."

Gita walked out of the library building slowly, her head bowed. Like an abandoned and battered dog, Leike thought as she watched her. She had known this day would come.

In the following days, the surviving members of Jonah's family gathered to discuss the situation. Steam rose from the teacups. They all felt responsible for Jonah's daughter, including Lazar, who had managed to escape Lithuania and was now living in the United States. His brother, Berke Goldberg, was the one who had tried to raise money to pay Stanislava, but came to the farm too late to redeem her.

There was much discussion about what to do—but the group couldn't even agree on what to call the girl. No one called her Gita, whether in conversation or in letters. She was simply referred to as "Jonah's daughter." Lazar was the only one who insisted on using her given name—Elida. "What about Elida, Jonah's daughter, may the Lord avenge his blood?" Lazar asked in every letter he sent from America.

AFTER MEETING LEIKE AT THE LIBRARY, GITA WAS EXhausted and became ill. She could not lift her head and her legs did not respond. She was cold and shivery.

All she could remember afterward was that an arm wrapped in a woolen sleeve, like that of Mame's coat, slipped under her arm and carried her on feathers. She felt nothing more than that. She lay on the couch for four days, trapped between the big pillow and the blanket. She was delirious with fever. "Mom, Mom," she exclaimed in Lithuanian, "Dad, Dad, what did they do to you? Why did you leave me? I want Mom! I want Dad!" Images of a burning town, a black forest and pits, a barn and frolicking animals, floated before her eyes. From a distance, voices came to her. Mame approached with a cup of tea and walked away, served kasha (porridge) and walked away. She heard them quarreling from afar. "Just trouble, just trouble," Tate muttered, and Mame cried. She noticed Dr. Lifshitz leaning over her and whispering, "Gitale, Gitale, everything will be fine. I'll make sure you get well." She slept for long hours, waking up intermittently, and when she wasn't delirious, she was silent.

When Gita recovered and Dr. Lifshitz announced that she was allowed to leave the house, she hurried to meet Leike at the library. She arrived very pale and immediately hugged Leike and rested her head on her shoulder.

"Ask me anything you want to know," Leike finally told her.

"You're related to my father, right?"

"Right," Leike replied. "I'm your father's cousin."

"Did you know him? Did you meet him? Did you meet my mother?"

Leike began talking. She told Jonah's daughter about her father, his kindness, that he had saved the lives of many patients as a doctor and stayed in the Kovno ghetto to tend to the sick. She also told her about her mother, Tzila. She explained to Gita that it was because her parents had loved her so much that they decided to give her to a good woman who took her far from the ghetto.

Gita listened quietly until this point. But when Leike told her about her transfer to the farm, she angrily blurted, "How could parents give away their child? Abandon her? How? I'll never forgive them for leaving me!"

How do you explain to a girl that if she had not been handed over, her fate would have been certain death? She now understood why many parents refrained from telling their children about the atrocities they had gone through. No one who had not experienced that hell would ever be able to understand. To Gita she said, "They loved you so much and wanted so much for you to live. It was the only way to ensure your survival."

AT THEIR NEXT MEETING, LEIKE TOLD HER ABOUT THE name her parents gave her—Elida. Gita liked the name Elida very much. That evening, she informed Mame and Tate that she wanted to be called Elida.

"Impossible!" cried Mame. Tate responded with two ringing slaps on Gita's cheek. With a burning cheek, Gita turned and hissed, "If you call me Gita, I won't answer."

"Get out of the house right now!" Tate shouted at her, and she headed straight back to Leike's house.

When Leike saw the hand marks on the girl's cheek, she was stunned.

"What happened?" she asked.

"I don't want to live in their house anymore. As of today, I will be Elida!" Leike sat her down in the kitchen and made tea for both of them. She sighed and said, "You'll be able to change your name, but I ask you to wait. You're registered at school and elsewhere as Gita Ruhin. Do you know what will happen if we change your name now? All sorts of officials from the authorities will start investigating why and where this name came from. In the meantime, you must not do anything without your parents' permission."

"I don't care about all that," she replied. "You can call me Elida, Berke can call me that, and his children can also call me Elida. Tate and Mame too." Leike assured the girl that, from then on, within the family they would call her Elida.

In the following days, when she visited Berke's family, she was introduced as Elida. At school, she was still called Gita.

SHE SPENT WEEKENDS WITH HER NEW FAMILY. THE cousins her age were not always happy to spend time with Elida because of her stubbornness and her need to win every game she played.

On clear days, when Berke and his family and friends went out to the riverbank, spread out a tablecloth, and laid out delicacies on it, the children noticed the special patience and compassion the adults showered upon her. Only in deference to their parents did they treat her with mercy and not completely reject her.

At Mame and Tate's house, everyone walked around in silence. Mame did not stop crying and constantly worked in the kitchen to prepare dishes that Gita loved. She talked little with Tate, who was so often angry, coughing loudly and grumbling about everything.

Whenever Mame addressed her as Gita or Gitale, the girl would not answer. But all her protests failed to convince Mame and Tate to call her Elida. She agreed to an unwritten compromise: Mame called her "my child" (*mein kind*) and Tate addressed her as "you" (*du*).

During Elida's visits with Leike and Berke, she heard about her other family members, including two of her father's sisters: Leah, who lived with her husband and their two children in Israel, and Sarah, who lived in Canada with her husband and kids.

She heard a lot about Lazar. "Lazar is not only your father's cousin," Leike said. "He was also his best friend. They went everywhere together. He was also with your father in the ghetto and was there when you were born. He lives in America now and has never forgotten you. In all of his letters to Berke, he asks about you. When Berke came to see you at school, it was so that he could write Lazar about you. And now he, together with the family in Israel, are doing everything to help Mame, Tate, and you get out of here. But no one should know about it. You're a smart girl. You understand what it means that no one should know."

"I want to be with my real family!"

"At the moment, that's impossible. Here you are registered as the Ruhins' daughter. But now there's a chance that things will change. Mame is from Poland, and whoever was a Polish citizen before the war may return there and from there you can now immigrate to Israel."

That connected with the words she heard Tate and Mame whispering to Ida and Asherke at home: Poland, Gomulka, travel, visa, and money. They needed money to carry out their plan to emigrate. After hearing about the plan to leave Vilna, she realized that this was how she could reach her real family, and she returned home with some hope.

IN THE SECOND HALF OF 1956, OTHER JEWS IN VILNA also became more hopeful. People whispered about the possibility of leaving for Poland and from there to Israel. The first to benefit were Jews who could prove they were Polish citizens before the war. The newly appointed prime minister of Poland, Vladislav Gomulka, signed an agreement with Khrushchev that allowed Polish citizens who had fled to the Soviet Union during the war to return to Poland. Jews who relinquished their Polish citizenship could then leave Poland for Israel under the auspices of the Jewish Agency nongovernmental organization.

One of Jonah's cousins, the well-known attorney and financier Isaac Kozlowski, saw that the new agreement offered a chance for Jonah's daughter to reunite with her family in Israel. He told Lazar and other family members: "It seems to me that the mother in the Ruhin family came from Poland. I can help them return to Poland, and from there they can immigrate to Israel."

Lazar and Kozlowski mobilized to help facilitate the Ruhins' emigration. Still, the process was complicated. Applicants had to fill out countless forms and give up their jobs and membership in the Communist Party. In addition, their children were expelled from schools and the youth movement. This was of little concern to Yocheved and Joel, who worked at home. In any case, Joel was hardly working due to his illness. The prospect of leaving boosted their mental and physical resilience.

Gita realized that it was important to stay close to Mame and Tate. She knew she had to stop yelling at them, making faces, and disappearing without permission.

During the Jewish holidays, Gita went to the synagogue with Berke's children. A crowd of people gathered outside but did not go in. She heard their conversations about Jews traveling on a special bus to the Polish border who were caught and sent to prison for forging documents and attempting to escape.

"We're traveling after the Jewish holidays," she told Ilonka.

"Who are 'we'?" Ilonka asked.

It was so hard for her to tell her she was leaving with Tate and Mame. The words lingered in her mouth until she finally said, "Me and my parents. My mother is Polish!"

"Traveling with the tailor dad?" Ilonka asked sarcastically. Elida did not answer.

Although the family's travel documents to Poland were legal, the rumors about buses being seized at the border stirred anxiety in the Ruhin family. At night, Gita dreamed of her father wrapping her in his white medical robe and slipping her through the window of a bus, and her falling. In another dream, she ran after a bus with Mame and Tate in it and saw Tate standing next to the driver, who was Asherke, and Tate shouted at him, "Don't stop for her. Let her stay behind." She woke up drenched in sweat and with a pounding heart.

Mame was also scared. There were nights when Gita heard her dragging her feet to the kitchen and back and mumbling in Yiddish, "Daddy, my daddy."

During the days, the house was full of activity. Mame packed belongings and clothes inside wooden boxes that were dragged up to the third floor.

The school principal called Gita to her office. "Gita Ruhin, I understand that you are going to Poland. I'm sorry that due to your departure from Lithuania you will no longer be able to be a student at our school. You have always been an excellent student. All the teachers at our school have recognized your talents, and I hope you will excel in Poland as well. I look forward to a bright future for you. Do not shy away from the culture and knowledge you have acquired here in the Russian school." At the end of her speech, the principal gave Gita a diploma with a list of the subjects she had studied and next to each of them the highest grade. Years later, she was still grateful to the teachers and the education she had acquired there.

At the farewell meetings with her father's family, everyone was excited. Clara, Berke's wife, made pastries. Berke stroked her head and gazed at her with his blue eyes. In caressing her, he also meant to convey his love to his sisters, whom Gita would meet in Israel, and to his brother, Lazar, who would surely come from America to meet her in Israel.

Leike wrote to Lazar:

> *Jonah's daughter's life is too hard to talk about in a letter. Stories about the ten years she spent with those who were supposed to be her parents should be told orally, as there are no words to express this briefly on paper. It took a long time for her to pour her heart out. The people she grew up with are very simple but also mean and cruel. Although they allowed her to study and provided her with food and clothing, they treated her brutally. They beat her and shouted at her. She never received any love from them.*

Still, Leike cautioned Lazar to be kind to the Ruhins. "Meet them partway," she wrote. She suggested that he send them some money to help them get by in Israel. "Clearly, there is much more to tell. I think in time Elida will tell you everything herself."

•

ON A COLD DECEMBER DAY IN 1956, THE RUHIN FAMILY boarded a train from Vilna to Warsaw. The water in the river had frozen and the treetops had turned white. The few people in the street were wrapped in their coats and wore woolen hats. They walked carefully on the sidewalks and did not lift their heads to look at the three people heading to the train with bags and suitcases.

Mame warned Gita not to slip on the sidewalk, and Tate demanded that she stop speaking Yiddish. Gita's body sagged under the weight of the suitcase she carried, and the straps of her backpack cut into her shoulders. Inside her socks, she felt the rustling of the dollars she had seen Berke give them. Before setting off on their trip, Mame had placed the stash of bills in her socks. "They won't suspect a child," she said. "It's money we need to have with us. Don't tell anyone!" She had also seen Tate unravel the hem of his coat and stuff it with money, rings, and Mame's necklace, which she had kept in the buffet and never wore around her neck.

On the last night, they slept on mattresses and covered themselves with their coats; the blankets were already packed. The echo in the empty apartment increased the feeling of anxiety, which had been her constant companion in recent weeks. She felt it in cramps in her intestines, in headaches, and in her quickened heartbeat. The last few nights, she had tossed and turned in her bed and could not fall asleep. Images of the Vilna market, the library, the street, the pharmacy, and the pharmacist appeared at a dizzying pace in her head. What would happen now when Leike could no longer look after her and protect her?

There were many families with children at the station, with a lot of packages and suitcases tied with ropes. "These are Poles returning to Poland, not all of them Jews," Mame explained to her. They entered a crowded hall and were directed by a Lithuanian in a dark uniform to a table, behind which sat a clerk, also in a dark uniform.

"Papers!" he demanded. The bundle of dollars in her socks rustled in her ears. The clerk checked the papers, instructed Mame and Tate to sign some forms, and studied Gita's face. "Are you Gita Ruhin? Their daughter?"

"Yes!" Mame exclaimed, pulling out a letter from the school. "Here, here it's written, Gita Ruhin! It's written here that she fulfilled all of her requirements at school." Mame also pulled out Gita's certificate of excellence. The clerk looked again at Gita's face and said, "Nice, nice," and turned to the next family.

They finally reached the platform. Gita's eyes wandered past the passengers huddled there and across the crowd moving toward the waiting train. There were small rectangular signs on the train cars indicating the destination. When they boarded the train, Mame pulled them toward the end of the car, where a family with two children had already settled. The eldest daughter seemed to be Gita's age.

"They're Jews," her mother whispered. Without waiting

for a response, Mame pressed forward, sat down next to the Jewish family, and motioned to Gita to join her.

"No," Gita insisted. "I'll sit there," she said, pointing to a bench in the middle of the car. "There's still room there."

THEY CROSSED THE BORDER AND THE LANGUAGE ON THE signs changed. The conductor announced the Warsaw station, and the train slowed down. The passengers stood up, reached for their bundles on the shelves above them, and prepared to disembark. Some bent down to peer out the windows and called out the names of streets and neighborhoods; there were also cries of sorrow. They reached an area where all the buildings had been destroyed, leaving behind only piles of red bricks. Workers stood among the ruins and watched the faces of the passengers pressing against the train windows.

Mame's mouth spouted a flood of sentences in Polish. The train's horn at the station signaled her homecoming. The refugees were directed to a hall where a row of clerks sat. Suddenly, a man wrapped in an elegant coat and a muffler around his neck crossed their path and stood next to them. "Jews?" he asked. Mame nodded her head, and the father of the other family did likewise. The man said a few sentences in Polish and gave a note to Mame and the head of the other family. With sparkling eyes, they nodded understandingly and shoved the notes into their pockets.

The Ruhins were then questioned for over an hour by

a clerk who reexamined their papers and scrutinized their faces. He pointed to Gita and asked, "Is this your daughter?" And Mame repeated, "*Tak, tak,*" and showed the form bearing the name Gita Ruhin.

Gita lowered her gaze and began to shuffle from side to side, wrapping her toes around the bag with the money inside her socks. Tate noticed the motion, walked over to her, and commanded in a menacing whisper, "Stand up straight!"

The process was finally over. When they left the station, they met the man who had approached them earlier. He led them safely through the streets over piles of building blocks. Warsaw looked like a large construction site, even more than Vilna had looked after the war. "Almost the whole city was destroyed in the war," their guide explained to them, "and now it is being rebuilt."

They came to a street where there were buildings with several floors and a plaza between them. Weeds and bushes sprouted between the tiles. "Here." The man pointed. From the stairwell emerged a slender, short man wearing a fur beret. "*Kom mit mir,*" he said in Yiddish, and led them to the third floor.

"You will be here until the travel documents to Israel arrive," the man told them. Gita saw Mame shoving green bills into his pocket. "Thank you, thank you," he said without looking at the bills, and left. After he left, Mame hurried to close the door.

This was a difficult time for Jews in Poland, even for those who adopted a Polish national identity and communism. With the rise of Gomulka to power, riots and demonstrations broke out. The focus of hatred was the Jews, who were now identified with the communist regime. Crowds of Poles marched on the main streets of Warsaw carrying anti-Semitic posters. The remnants of Polish Jewry—thirty thousand in all, most of them Holocaust survivors, including many who had abandoned their Judaism—read in horror the signs saying: "Hitler killed communists and Jews and we'll finish the job!" Thousands lined the doors of the Israeli embassy in Warsaw, turned in their party membership cards, and hurried to exploit the opportunity to immigrate to Israel.

The Ruhin family was already registered as slated for immigration to Israel. The small family had received a "blue card," a temporary ID for those who had given up their citizenship and were about to leave the Soviet Union or Poland. The visas sent by Gita's family in Israel were issued on the pretense of family reunification: a document signed by a lawyer in Haifa claimed that Yocheved was related to Leah Spiegel, one of Jonah's sisters.

In February 1957, Mame was informed that they would leave Warsaw for Vienna in March, and there they would be told how to proceed to Israel. The Israeli embassy official turned to Gita and said, solemnly, "There will soon be an end to your journey, and you'll be an Israeli in the land of Israel!" The phrase "There will soon be an end" was etched in Gita's head. The word "end" has many meanings. What did it mean for her?

•

A JEWISH AGENCY OFFICIAL MET THEM UPON THEIR arrival in Vienna and brought them to a guesthouse. "You'll stay here for a few days," he explained. She noticed that the Israeli officials they encountered looked different than the Jewish refugees. The Israelis walked around handing out instructions, exuding self-confidence, while the refugee Jews humbly complied, responding with tired smiles. Elida tried to catch the Hebrew words that occasionally popped up in the Israelis' speech. When they were in Warsaw, they had gathered the children, divided them into groups, and started teaching them Hebrew. Leike had told her that Jonah spoke Hebrew, so she also wanted to learn that language.

A few days later, they boarded another train. The landscape they passed changed. Now they saw high mountains with white peaks and towns with houses topped by snow-covered roofs. "We're crossing the Alps in both Austria and Italy," Gita heard a father explain to his child. Again, the map hanging on the school wall came to mind.

As they moved south, her mood improved. Tate and Mame also seemed calmer. Perhaps their suffering would come to an end in Israel.

Excitement surged as the train slowed down and entered the city of Genoa. The passengers had some time to wander among the market stalls before boarding a Haifa-bound ship for the last leg of their journey.

As the ship left Genoa, Gita watched the line of white foam stretching from the receding continent all the way to the ship. Once before she had seen a sea, when she traveled one summer to the shores of the Baltic Sea, and she had loved it. The sea called out to her. She imagined herself sinking into the blue-green abyss.

4

Elida with the Family, Haifa

On the last day of the voyage to Israel, there was a flurry of activity on the ship.

"Wear your warm clothes, it may be cold when we get there," Mame said as she riffled through the suitcases.

Elida looked mockingly at Mame. "It's already April and summer is here soon. It's hot in Israel and we won't need the warm clothes."

Mame folded and unfolded the clothes. The wind on board and her experience had taught her that when arriving at a new place it was most important to stock up on warm clothes.

"At least take a sweater with you, just in case," she said.

Impatiently, Elida took the sweater Mame had knitted for her and hurried up to the deck.

The ship approached the wharf with horns blaring. The group roared excitedly, "Land! The land of Israel! Haifa!" Mount Carmel stood proudly before their eyes. The day was bright, and the sun shone on the water and on the amazed faces of the passengers.

Elida studied the view, her eyes drawn to a shimmering golden dome in the center of the slope. For a moment, a thought crossed her mind: Are there churches here? Here, in the land of the Jews? She observed the passengers and noticed tears streaming down some of their faces. She looked for Mame and Tate. Suddenly filled with tender feelings toward Mame, she felt the need to stand by her. Mame had assured her that they would come here, and now they had arrived. She noticed that Mame had tears in her eyes.

The descent ramp was connected to the ship and the passengers began to squeeze together to disembark. When they reached the platform, everyone scurried to and fro. An official, speaking Hebrew and Yiddish, urged them to proceed toward a wooden hut. In the hut, clerks sat at wooden tables handling dozens of sheets of paper. Occasionally, they blue-stamped a sheet and moved on to a new pile of forms. Elida immediately realized that they were deciding where to send the new immigrants. She knew that her real family lived in Haifa, so she stood in front of Mame and listened closely.

"Is this your daughter?" a clerk asked as he looked at Elida.

"Yes," Mame replied.

"And your family lives in Haifa? The family that sent you the request to reunite relatives?"

"Yes, yes," Elida answered immediately. "They are here in Haifa, and we want to live near them," she added without being asked.

"Oh, I see you have a wise assistant," the clerk said, examining Tate's pale, silent face with interest. "So again, what's your name? When were you born? Where are the certificates?"

Elida remembered the instructions well. She must consistently be Gita Ruhin, these are her parents, she was born in Russia during the war, and thus her papers and documents were written later.

The clerk continued to flip through the papers, looked at Gita and her parents, and nodded. "You're lucky, there are still houses left here in Kiryat Haim, near Haifa," he said.

"What do you mean near Haifa, how far is it?" Elida asked. The clerk was impressed by the girl's determination.

"I need to get approval from my supervisor," he said in Yiddish. As he walked over to the supervisor, he felt the girl's gaze on his back. He soon returned with a small smile on his face and said, "Yes, Kiryat Haim. Don't worry, it's very close to Haifa. Go with the papers and they'll take you to your new home. Welcome!"

They went out to the square in front of the harbor. Elida was looking for her aunt. "Elida! My girl! Elida!" a woman cried as she ran toward Elida and embraced her. She backed away a little, examined her, and hugged her again. "I'm your aunt Leah, Jonah's sister. Oh, what happiness!" Beside her stood a handsome man with light-brown eyes and silver streaks in his hair. "This is my husband, Moshe, your uncle." Moshe smiled at Elida and said in Hebrew, "Welcome!" And then he welcomed Mame and Tate in Polish and Yiddish.

Her aunt calling her "Elida" signified the acceptance of her new identity. She was no longer Gita. Now there will be someone to take care of me, Elida thought. Now my real family is with me.

"Do you live close to here?" she asked her aunt.

"Yes, quite close to here and you'll be living not far from me. We can meet whenever you want," she replied.

"Can I come with you to your house right now?" Elida asked, hoping that Leah would call her by her name again.

"In a few days. Now go with them." It was clear that she was debating what to call her niece's parents. She knew that Elida had not been happy in her life with them, but she knew they had tried, and she felt sorry for them.

On the bus to Kiryat Haim, Elida stared out of the dusty window. The excitement and talk of the other passengers did not interest her. She tried to take in the sights along the way. When they left Haifa, the mountainside came into view, and a curved bay could be seen in the distance. The bus entered a small town with straight streets and modest houses. Kids were running everywhere. The immigrants in the bus got up and stretched their necks toward the windows. "This is Kiryat Haim, this is where we live!" they said with a mixture of fear, surprise, and wonder.

The bus turned onto a narrow road and stopped. "This is your neighborhood," the driver announced.

A row of houses stood in front of them. "This is our immigrant quarter," someone declared. The sight was unlike anything Elida had seen so far. A row of houses planted in a sea of bright sand. Fuel tanks and an industrial building that emitted smoke stood some distance away. The immigrants quickly collected their belongings and hurried the children along.

Their new apartment was in the sixth house in the row. It included a kitchenette, toilet, and two small rooms. Along the walls stood iron beds with mattresses, a wooden table, and chairs. There was an aluminum kettle on the counter in the kitchenette.

"The toilets are inside!" Mame exclaimed. She went and flushed the toilet in amazement. "There is also running water to shower. When our belongings arrive, it will be even better."

Tate was pale and had difficulty breathing. "Now I want a cup of tea and a nap. There's plenty of time to see everything and get organized."

Elida went out into the yard. I'm leaving, she thought, I'm not staying with them. I will have another home. I need to convince my aunt and Mame that everyone will be better off if I live with my real family.

•

THE FIRST DAYS IN THEIR NEW HOME IN ISRAEL WERE UNsettling for the Ruhin family. Tate had difficulty breathing as he lay in the narrow iron bed. A warm sea breeze blew in through the window. Mame was busy organizing their belongings and clothes and occasionally went out to ask the neighbors where to buy things. They had also heard about Israel's network of health clinics during the journey. It was important for her to find a local clinic because of her husband's medical condition.

Elida insisted on seeing her new home as temporary. Throughout her trip to Israel, she had imagined the meeting with her family in Haifa, entering her aunt's house, the hug she would get from her. She would go back to school; she was told there were good schools in Israel. She envisioned living in a house in Haifa on the mountain slope, and she dreamed of walking on the beach at the seashore. The Hebrew language did not intimidate her. She recognized words from Yiddish and reassured herself that her family knew Yiddish and would understand her. They would also get to know her and see how talented she was at learning languages. It was harder for her to imagine how she would finally break away from her parents and how she would move on to live with her own family. There were times when she was filled with pity for Mame, but she would quickly convince herself that they would live near each other and that she would visit Mame often.

The day after they arrived in Kiryat Haim, Aunt Leah came with her husband, Moshe, and their two children. Mame was in her house robe and apron and was rummaging through the clothes in the suitcases. Tate was sitting in a chair in the entrance, fanning himself with the Yiddish newspaper. Elida was sitting on a stone in the backyard, looking out at the sandy surroundings.

When she heard her aunt's voice, she hurried back into the apartment. "Elida, dear girl." Leah moved toward her. "Come and meet the family. This is my daughter, Rochale, she's your age, and this is my son, Muki." Elida reached out her hand to them. Unconsciously pulling down the plaid dress with the collar, she sought to hide her legs with the ungainly shoes and stockings up to her knees.

Rochale wore a blue bell skirt and a thin white blouse. Her long hair was fastened with hair clips on both sides. She wore sandals on her feet. Elida felt awkward compared to her. Rochale smiled and said, "Hello and welcome," but found no more words.

"Come, come," cried Leah, "I brought you a new blouse, like Rochale's. Do you know who Rachel was? She was your father's mother and mine, your grandmother, so I named my daughter after her."

Rochale tried to converse with Elida in Hebrew, but she ran out of words very quickly. Elida was more interested in the conversation of the adults, thinking that perhaps they would talk about her. But her name was not mentioned.

"When will I come to you?" she dared to ask Leah before she left.

"In a few days you'll come and meet your other aunts and uncles."

Leah told Mame about Holocaust Remembrance Day the following day, and they talked about the catastrophe. "The most important thing is that we now have our own country," Leah said. "You'll see how good it is that we have a state of our own, and how important it is that you came here. Independence Day will be in a week. Come visit us in Haifa and see how beautiful and happy it will be."

"We'll see, we'll see," said Mame. "Meanwhile, it's difficult and hot and Joel is not feeling well."

Elida was upset that the invitation was not addressed just to her. She wanted to be alone with her family. "I'll come alone!" she announced, almost shouting.

"We'll have to teach you how to get to us by bus," Leah said.

"How? Alone? She doesn't know where to go and doesn't speak Hebrew," Mame protested.

"The first time I'll come to pick her up and then it'll be simpler," Leah concluded.

The conversation depressed Elida. She bowed her head and fell silent. They want me to stay here in Kiryat Haim, with Tate and Mame, she thought. No one is talking about me living in Haifa with my family.

Leah noticed her distress and tried to encourage her. "Do you know the significance of our holiday, Independence Day? It's a holiday that marks the establishment of the State of Israel. There will be dancing in the streets, army parades, bonfires."

Elida was not interested in the holiday and did not understand her aunt's excitement. On the way to Israel, the emissaries tried to make the young immigrants proud of the new country. She knew all about these kinds of celebrations—with red flags and enthusiastic speeches praising communism. Such ceremonies would not help her feel at home. She wanted a family.

In the days following the visit, the skies turned gray, matching her somber mood, and a heavy rain fell. "This is an unusual phenomenon," they said on the street in Kiryat Haim. "Who ever heard of rain in May?" The rainwater leaked into their small apartment, and Mame feared the moisture would harm Tate. Elida refused to go to the school in Kiryat Haim to attend special Hebrew classes for new immigrants. "I'm older than they are and what they learn bores me." Everything around her was depressing—the sands, the people, and the bleakness in the small apartment.

ON THE EVE OF INDEPENDENCE DAY, LEAH CAME TO TAKE Elida to her home in Haifa. Elida's suitcase was already packed. Leah had agreed in advance with Mame that she would take Elida for a few days.

Tate uttered a weak goodbye. Mame was still trying to adjust the dress Elida wore. "We sewed this for her," she announced proudly.

The journey to Haifa by bus took about an hour. Blue-and-white flags with a blue Star of David in the center fluttered along the streets. In some places, schoolchildren marched with white T-shirts, holding Israeli flags in their hands. Leah was proud and never stopped drawing Elida's attention to flags and people, trying to make her niece feel her pride. This is the daughter of Jonah, her beloved brother who was murdered. If he had only come to the homeland before the catastrophe, as she had, everything would have been different.

"Do you know that your father knew Hebrew very well? He wrote the letters he sent me before the war only in Hebrew. He was a Zionist, and he would surely have been proud to know that you're here."

They reached Herzl Street and walked to Leah's house. Her eyes fell upon the rows of shops whose windows displayed clothes, housewares, books, and fabrics. The names were written in Hebrew, and she quietly deciphered them. The shopkeepers had hung flags in the shop windows. There were stone houses of several stories, with balconies, and sidewalks ran alongside the paved roads bustling with cars and the sound of honking horns. A city! So different from the sandy area where the house in Kiryat Haim stood.

"Come, come," said Leah, noticing a slight change in Elida. "Here is your uncle Pinchas's shop. He helped a lot in bringing you to Israel, and this is your aunt Yehudit. She's your father's cousin."

"She looks just like Jonah." Yehudit sighed. "This is a good day to come to us, a holiday. How are you doing?" she asked in Yiddish.

Later, Elida would learn that Pinchas's store served as

the family's center. He was the one who arranged things for everyone.

Leah's house stood at the end of an alley near the store, in a white three-story stone building. Leah lived upstairs. When Elida entered the apartment, she could hardly refrain from bursting into tears. How different it was from their apartment in Kiryat Haim! A polished white kitchen, a living room with dining table and chairs, three large and spacious rooms with high ceilings and toilets. How nice it was to go out onto the porch, which overlooked a multi-story school that had wide windows and a very large yard.

"That's the Alliance school," Leah explained. "My Muki is in elementary school and Rochale will be in high school there next year."

School! A few months had passed since she left Vilna and her school. How she missed the organized lessons, the teachers, and the library. She wanted to continue studying at a school like that, with a respectable building and an inviting yard, unlike the one in Kiryat Haim, where they wanted her to learn Hebrew with younger children in a building that was nothing like any school she had known.

In the evening, before the festivities, the house was abuzz. Rochale was getting ready to go out to celebrate with her Scout group. "We'll go to Herzl Street soon, too, and meet Rochale," Leah told Elida.

The streets were crowded with people. Groups of children of all ages held hands and marched in a line as they made their way between the celebrants. She felt overwhelmed by the noise and congestion but didn't dare to say anything to Leah, who was holding her hand. Songs were broadcast on loudspeakers and circles of dancers formed in the middle of the streets. Boys and girls in shorts and sandals hopped and sang, dancing and dancing. Elida had to admit to herself that they really looked happy. But they were so different from her, and she felt no desire to connect with them.

Moshe noticed her embarrassment. "Well, that's enough, let's go. I see Elida is tired."

Elida was glad and nodded at his offer to go home.

But Leah was not ready to go home yet. "Come, I'll buy you some ice cream," she said, pulling Elida toward a stand where a large group of people had gathered. Those who asked loudest were served ice cream that dripped over the heads of those waiting their turn. After finishing their ice cream, Leah announced, "We're going to a party now at Yaffa and David's apartment; they're your aunt and uncle too."

The apartment was crowded with more than twenty people, all dressed in festive clothes. The men and women, who looked the same age as Leah and Moshe, sang songs in Hebrew and Yiddish. When she entered, she was smothered by Aunt Yaffa and Aunt Hannah, who told her that they were also her father's cousins, like Yehudit. Yehudit and Pinchas were there too.

Elida was introduced and received a cheerful welcome from the entire group. Two of the men started talking to her in Lithuanian. "Most of us here came from Lithuania," they explained to her. In the company of the adults, she felt more relaxed. The atmosphere delighted her. She was happy to be the center of attention. The Yiddish she knew rolled off their tongues. But there were those who insisted: "In our country we speak Hebrew." It was already late at night, but the group did not stop dancing and singing.

The next day, she was taken to Herzl Street to watch the parade. The loudspeakers played songs, and rows of teens dressed in white shirts, with the boys in blue pants and the girls in blue skirts, marched, sang, and danced.

"Beautiful, isn't it?" Leah pressed her, in the hope that the cheerfulness around her would awaken a spark of joy in the dejected girl, and that a glimmer of light would shine in her gloomy eyes.

THE DAYS AFTER INDEPENDENCE DAY WERE NOT EASY. Elida shuttled between Kiryat Haim and her aunt's house, all the while demanding to move in with her in Haifa. "I want my family," she snapped at Mame.

"And are they prepared for you to move in?" Mame challenged her.

When the voices grew in volume, Tate intervened, banged on the table, and shouted, "Let her go! How long can we hold on to a girl who does not want us?"

Social workers were assigned to check on the new immigrants. Bella, a Yiddish-speaking social worker, entered the Ruhin family home. She sat with Elida and Mame while Tate sat on the side and listened.

"I want to talk about your daughter, Gita," she said after spreading the papers on her lap. Mame fell silent.

Elida's body stiffened. Should she tell her story or was it still dangerous to reveal the truth about her life? Did she still have to hide her real name? Throughout the journey she had agreed to be called Gita and did not tell anyone that Mame and Tate were not her real parents. Maybe it was now time to expose the story?

"It's written in our papers that Gita does not go to school. The details about her age are also not clear. If there's a problem, maybe I can help."

Bella's pleasant voice broke the dam holding back Elida's words, which started in a careful trickle and soon became a torrent. "I have another name. My name is Elida, not Gita.

"My name is Elida because that's what my real mother and father called me. My father, Jonah Freidman, was a doctor in the Kovno ghetto, where I was born. My mother was called Tzila. My parents died in the ghetto, and they"—she pointed her finger—"took me in after the war and did not tell me anything. They called me Gita and didn't tell me that I had another mother who gave birth to me and another father. Only about a year ago, I found out for myself and then I also wanted them to call me Elida, the name my parents gave me. I have uncles and aunts from my father's family here and also an aunt who is my father's sister and I want to go back to my family. I want to go and live with my aunt in Haifa."

"It's not that simple," Bella said. "You have to go to school here and learn Hebrew. Maybe in time the difficulties will disappear. The first months are not easy for any of the immigrants."

"I want to study in Haifa, not here. Can that be arranged?"

"I'm not sure, because you're listed here. First, try to learn Hebrew here."

"She's a very talented and smart girl," Mame said proudly. "You should see her grades, the certificates of excellence. She already speaks some Hebrew because she learned it on the way with the teachers from the Jewish Agency."

Elida raised her head. Though she was accustomed to Mame's praise and sometimes even angry at her bragging, this time she straightened up a little where she sat, so that Bella would know she was not a simpleton. A tiny smile flickered on her lips.

When she said goodbye to the members of the Ruhin family, Bella did not promise them anything. She knew for sure that more meetings were still in store for them and that Elida's story would eventually reach the courts.

Leah also understood Elida's difficulties, her longing for change, and her desire to live with Jonah's family. She went to Kiryat Haim to talk to the Ruhins and ask their permission to send Elida to Geula School, where her cousins studied. "It will calm her down," she said apprehensively.

During that visit she realized that Mame had almost given up on Elida. "I have no more strength for arguments and battles from all directions," Mame lamented. "Joel is sick, he can't work, and I'm looking for work so that we have something to live on. The heat here is not good for me. I'm tired of quarreling with the girl. It's best for her to go to the school she wants. If it's in Haifa, then let it be in Haifa. For her, studies are the most important thing."

And so Leah enrolled Elida at Geula School. But she was unsuccessful in persuading Elida's cousins—Zipi, Nili, and Rochale—to include her in their games during recess at school. The connections between them existed only when she visited their homes. Elida grasped the difference between her and her cousins. They were cheerful and free girls who spent time with their peers. The chasm between them was deep and the few words she knew in Hebrew could not bridge it.

When do they read books? she wondered. Although there was a bookcase in each house laden with many rows of books, she had never seen them read.

"Do you have a library?" she asked Zipi, the daughter of Pinchas and Yehudit. "Do you read books?"

"Sure," she replied.

"Can I come with you to the library?"

Zipi agreed to take her to the library on Pevzner Street. In the library, Elida found several shelves with books in Russian. She stood in front of the shelves, tilted her head to read the names of the books, reached out, and moved her hand along the length of each shelf. Zipi had already chosen a book and showed Elida, *Little Women*. "I'm taking this book for the second time." Elida reluctantly left the library with her.

"How do I register? How can I get books?" she asked.

"You have to sign up; it costs money," Zipi informed her.

The next day Leah took her to the library and registered her. "Perhaps you should try books in Hebrew and not Russian?" she asked, but Elida rejected the offer. She chose *War and Peace* by Tolstoy.

"Are these the books you read?"

"Sure, I've read some of it before."

Eventually, it was agreed that Elida should live with Leah and Moshe in Haifa and go to school there. Leah was pleased but also worried. She loved Elida, but she was a difficult girl and would take attention away from her own children. Plus, the family was in dire financial straits at the time.

But still there were so many bright moments. Seven-year-old Muki became attached to Elida. She taught him to play chess and helped him improve his arithmetic, often giving him mathematical riddles.

Leah made sure Elida's new clothes were the same as Rochale's. She sewed blue jumper dresses and matching white blouses for both of them and bought them the same pair of sandals. The two girls were photographed in the same attire and the photo was sent to relatives in Texas, Canada, and Vilna.

•

LAZAR GOLDBERG FLED FROM LITHUANIA AT THE END OF the war and settled in Texas with his wife, Toibeh, and three of his brothers. He became a wealthy merchant and a respected man in the local Jewish community. However, his status did not erase the memory of the dark days in the ghetto, the horrors of war, and the covenant he had made with his cousin and soul mate, Jonah. From a distance, he followed Elida's fate. Through his brother Berke, he sent money to the Ruhin family and his assistance enabled them to travel to Poland. His brother-in-law Pinchas did everything necessary to supply the Ruhin family with all the necessary papers to get to Israel.

From far away, Lazar excitedly received the news of Elida's arrival in Israel and planned to meet her. In a conversation with Toibeh, which lasted deep into the night, they decided that he would adopt Elida and bring her to the United States. To his sisters in Israel, he wrote:

> *Toibeh and I want to bring Jonah's daughter to us, so that she will be our daughter. We have failed to bring children into the world, nor will we in the future. Inwardly, I always knew that the time would come when I would be able to fulfill my promise to Jonah. I've sat on the sidelines and let the poor girl suffer for too long. Now that the girl has managed to get out of Vilna, I will bring her to*

me, and she will be our daughter. Perhaps this will ease my conscience, even if only a little, for abandoning Jonah and Tzila there in the ghetto.

Lazar arrived in Israel in July 1957, intent on fulfilling his covenant with Jonah. His first meeting with Elida took place at Leah's home. Elida was eager to meet him, but she was also anxious. She recognized him from the photographs—wavy hair gathered back, blue eyes, thick lips, and protruding teeth—and she knew he was the one who had helped bring her to Israel.

Lazar stood with tears in his eyes. He hugged her and sobbed, "*Meidele,* my girl. Where are you, Jonah? What happened to us? If you only knew. Jonah," he whimpered. He sat down on a chair and held his head between his palms, his shoulders shaking with his sobs.

Elida stood in front of him, embarrassed. She could not comprehend how badly shaken this man was. She could not know that he was remembering Jonah carrying her in his arms and delivering the basket beyond the ghetto fence, his tear-streaked face hidden under a hat; the dark alleys; the smell of death. The words of his covenant with Jonah were etched in his memory: "If one of us does not survive, we will adopt the other's children and raise them like our own. We will be their parents and will love them as if they were our own flesh and blood."

In the days that followed, Lazar clung to Elida but did not share these dark memories with her. "She has known enough sadness and sorrow. Now she will be my daughter!" he resolved.

At night, lying on the folding bed that Leah opened for her every evening, Elida stared at the high white ceiling. The image of her uncle with his hands covering his eyes came to her again. She had become accustomed to tears, but she had never encountered such a sight as her uncle sobbing like that.

What is it about her that makes everybody cry? The behavior of the adults frightened her. She felt they were expecting something from her that she could not give them. With Tate and Mame, she had to be what they wanted her to be. Here, everyone wanted her to love everyone, to admire their country, to be like Rochale or Nili. And now they wanted her to immediately love the uncle who came from America.

I'm mature enough to know what I want, she thought, sighing, rolling over in her bed. When she fell asleep, she dreamed that she was in the yard of the house in Kiryat Haim. Mame, Tate, Lazar, Leah, and Pinchas were in the apartment, along with other people she did not recognize. Everyone was speaking in whispers. Elida knew for sure that they were talking about her. She turned her back and started running. Mame and Lazar ran after her and grabbed her from both sides. The three of them ascended to heaven, and the people below looked up toward them, shading their eyes. Suddenly, she let go of their hands and started plummeting toward the ground. The feeling of falling was clear and sharp, and she awoke with a cry.

The next day, Lazar took Elida and her cousins on a shopping spree, as he had done on his previous visits to Israel. They entered a children's clothing store and he said, "Choose whatever you want." While they were inspecting the clothes, he chatted with the owner of the store. When he was in Israel, he never missed an opportunity to speak fluent Hebrew with everyone he met.

Elida was disappointed that she had to share his attention with the whole gang. The clothes looked childish to her. The girls chose shorts and T-shirts. But Elida preferred the dresses and jumpers Mame had made for her. They won't force me to dress like them and behave like them, she vowed. While Elida was looking at the dresses in the store, Zipi called out to her with a laugh, "Not those Diaspora dresses anymore, it's enough. Get shorts, it is summer now!" The girls' giggles angered her, and she bolted from the store. Lazar hurried after her. "What happened?" he asked.

"I already have enough clothes," she replied, without looking up at him. He went inside, hurried the girls to finish their shopping, paid, and went out to her again.

The group of children disturbed Elida. She wanted Lazar for herself. He had only been in the country for a few days, but she had already learned that it was his custom to gather all the children of his extended family and take them with him everywhere. They were all his sons and daughters, the answer to his longings.

Still, Elida soon became attached to Lazar. She met with him every day and not always with the other children.

They would go to the ice cream stand or get corn on the cob. A fat, sweaty man would pull the steaming corn from a vat and place it on green corn leaves. When she agreed to taste the delicacy that all the children were lining up to buy, she burned her lips.

From time to time, the whole family traveled by bus to Mount Carmel. They sat at wooden tables in a tavern; the adults talked, and the children played. In the sparse pine grove, Elida longed for the forests of Vilna. Those were real forests. She did not understand how the adults who grew up in Lithuania could be proud of this modest forest.

In the evenings, the adults gathered on the balconies and spoke Yiddish. They could sit like that for hours every evening and talk; they always had something to talk about. Elida preferred their company. Her command of Yiddish and closeness to Lazar made it more enjoyable than spending time with the children in the family. In their conversations on the balconies, she heard about life in America, about the shops and trade with the Mexicans, and about each one of her cousins in America. She heard about politics in Israel, listened to debates about the Labor Party, which Pinchas reviled, and about the Herut Party and Mr. Begin, whom Yaffa adored.

One Saturday, Elida met Avigdor for the first time. He was a soldier, Pinchas and Yehudit's son. When Lazar saw him in uniform, he began weeping again—though he wept for a different reason this time: he was overcome with pride. "He fought in Sinai in the war a year ago," Lazar noted.

One morning, after an evening that involved much whispering, Elida sat with Leah and asked, "What are you hiding from me? I want to live with you and be your daughter."

"You must understand, Elida, things are not that simple. We're considering what will happen to you in the future and we're exploring all sorts of options."

"What options? Are you deciding for me?" she asked angrily. "I will not return to Kiryat Haim. You promised me that you'd take care of me. You're my father's sister. You promised me that I'd have a family here that would take care of me."

Leah, who had been standing until then, pulled up a chair and sat down facing Elida. "I want to ask you something. Are you prepared to travel with Lazar to America and be his daughter? He and his wife, Toibeh, want to adopt you and take you to live with them. Are you willing to go?"

There was silence. Elida could feel her heart beating. Lazar? America? How had she failed to realize that this was why he had come? He really cared about her, was good and nice, but go to America?

Leah's heart also accelerated. She was not supposed to tell Elida about the plan. But now, she felt she could hide it from her no longer. She's right, we have to share it with her. Leah noticed the astonishment that gripped Elida and anticipated the next blow, which was indeed not late in coming.

"You're getting rid of me again, like some package being

handed from family to family. I so much wanted to come here, to live with my family."

"No one is getting rid of you. We just want the best for you. If all goes well, you'll see that this is the best thing for you."

"Best for me?" She got up angrily. The chair fell. She hurried out of Leah's apartment.

Leah ran after her. "Wait, where are you going? Let's sit down and talk."

Elida quickly ran down the stairs, floor after floor. Tears washed down her face. In her mind, Herzl Street had changed into the street where she lived in Vilna, where she had fled to escape Tate's wrath.

Leah hurriedly changed out of her house robe and into a dress, grabbed her purse, and ran downstairs, hoping to find Elida in the yard. But Elida had disappeared from sight, and Leah hurried to Pinchas's shop to consult with him.

"Children who've experienced what she's been through are difficult," Pinchas noted. "She'll calm down and come back. But now you have to act wisely," he cautioned Leah.

Elida walked toward Gan Binyamin and from there turned to the library, where she could sit in the reading room, relax, and think. Dickens's *David Copperfield* came to mind. He ran away from his stepfather to his aunt Betsy, who took him into her house. But she had run to her aunt and was now being sent elsewhere.

"*David Copperfield?*" the librarian asked. "We only have it in Hebrew. Maybe you should try it. It's in a big font.

The kids here read it a lot. Try it." Why not try? She needed to learn to read Hebrew if she was going to live in Israel.

She took the book in Hebrew and left the library.

After calming down a bit, Elida arrived at her aunt Yaffa's home with the book in her hands. Yaffa gave her something to eat, her regular remedy for all pains. "What happened?" she asked gently, and then listened to Elida's emotional account, including her accusations that the family was insensitive to her troubles.

Yaffa placed her hand on Elida's arm. "You're upset and I understand you. We all understand you, and that's why we're only thinking about what's best for you. Lazar will talk to you and explain why he wants you to come with him and you'll tell him what you think and how you feel, and then we'll see."

Some family members were reluctant to send her to America: "The poor girl wants to be with Leah. She regards her as the mother she never had. And now we'll send her to the other end of the world? It's too harsh . . . We mustn't disappoint her after everything she's been through, now that she's finally arrived in Israel . . . You can't decide for her, you have to ask her what she wants, she'll take it hard . . . Her tough life has made her bitter and angry. Lazar and Toibeh will have a hard time raising her."

Various family members presented these and other arguments, but Lazar rejected them all. "I want to adopt Elida," he insisted. "Since I left Kovno, I've lived with the hope that I can fulfill my promise to Jonah. God has granted me the financial wherewithal to provide children with the very best opportunities but has denied me children of my own. Toibeh and I have decided that Elida will be our daughter."

The next day, Lazar picked up Elida in a taxi, and they drove together to the Shavei Zion Hotel on the beach. There, as they walked leisurely along the rocky shore, to the soothing sound of the waves, he told her about the special connection he had with her father, how they grew up together, studied together at the Hebrew Culture School, and made Hebrew the language of communication between them. They started medical school together, but he had been forced to leave after two years because of financial difficulties. He said the whole family was proud of her father's success. Lazar also praised Elida for inheriting her father's abilities and for excelling as he had. He told her what a good man and a devoted doctor he was, and how he helped people in the ghetto.

That night, lying between the white sheets in her bed, Elida saw her father in a medical robe as in the picture at Leah's house. She saw Mame show her a new dress she had sewn for her, and Mame's worried face when she was sick. Elida also saw the pictures from Lazar's album—his wife in fancy clothes next to a big car, and a picture of her class at Geula School in Haifa. All these images danced before her and combined together. They demanded that she choose one of them, like a card drawn from a pile.

The next day, they continued their conversation. Lazar told her about his life in Laredo, about his brothers and their children, about the store, about his wife, Toibeh, who really wanted her to be with them. "You'll learn English, you'll have friends, and we'll buy you beautiful clothes. In a year, you'll be able to drive your own car."

She felt he was trying to tantalize her with material temptations and refused to immediately give her consent.

The open sea stretched out before her. Haifa was on the horizon, at the end of the bay. She remembered the view she had seen from the ship when they arrived in Haifa and thought to herself how different it was when viewed from Mount Carmel. There was something both alluring and terrifying about the sea.

Lazar quietly explained to her that the adoption procedure would take a long time, with many legal steps to complete before she could formally become his daughter. There was a good chance that the Ruhins would agree to the arrangement, he added.

Elida then replied, weighing each word: "If all goes well . . . if I don't have to change names . . . if I am Elida Goldberg, your daughter and Toibeh's, then I will come with you to America. But only on condition that you consider my wishes!"

Lazar hugged her, and she felt a warm tear on her cheek. Hers or his?

LAZAR WENT TO DISCUSS THE PLAN WITH JOEL AND Yocheved Ruhin. This was not their first meeting. As soon as he had arrived in Israel, Lazar had gone to visit them in Kiryat Haim. Their glum faces made him very sad. He brought gifts from America and bought them groceries. Mame hovered around the distinguished guest. He was no stranger to them; he was the one who had transferred money to them through his brother Berke, the money that allowed them to leave Vilna and come to Israel. They knew a lot about his concern and the responsibility he felt toward their child. They talked about Lithuania and what they had gone through in the war and wiped away tears for their children, Duvidl and Moishele.

Now, at this meeting, with Pinchas and Leah by his side, Lazar presented his request to legally adopt Elida. He observed the shabby furniture, Joel's pale face, Yocheved's sweaty, sad face, and a wave of pity flooded him. However, he felt that their situation actually reinforced his decision. There was no doubt that Jonah's girl deserved a different life.

"I want to take Elida with me to America. I know how hard it'll be for you after all these years of having a daughter, after all you've invested in her. You gave her a home, food, clothes, and schooling. You fulfilled her parents' request to give her a Jewish life." Yocheved nodded her head, confirming every detail that connected her to her Gita. Lazar felt he had to soften the bitterness and anger as much as possible.

The Ruhin couple had already come to terms with the fact that the girl would leave them. Still, Yocheved hoped that Elida would live in Haifa with Leah so that she could continue to see her. The possibility that the girl would move to America had never occurred to her. She began to cry, "What more is God asking of me?"

Lazar paused and waited for her to continue. She lamented quietly, in a mournful voice, "Why to America? Why not to Leah? Here at least I will not lose her. Here I can meet her, celebrate the holidays together as a family. We're a family after all these years. What will we do when she's in America? Will I see her grow up? How can I say goodbye to her?"

Joel was seething with rage and finally erupted: "What do you think? That you can just play with us? We raised the girl! To raise her in a Jewish family we paid the Gentile from the farm a lot of money! Also, for food, for doctors because she was often sick. Vacations, books, lots of books! We came here so she could see her family. Yocheved gave her everything a good mother can give." He banged the table angrily as he finished his tirade.

Leah sighed and added, "The decision to let her leave is hard for me too. For years, I waited for my brother's daughter to come here to grow up with me. I'm the closest family relation. I owe it to my brother. But I cannot give the girl what she needs: attention, financial support, studies that will suit her many abilities. Only Lazar can give her everything she needs today. There, in America, she will be sent to the best schools. We must not be selfish. We must give the girl the best, and in my situation today, I cannot."

"Lazar can send you money for her," Yocheved suggested.

Lazar interrupted her. "It's not only a matter of money. I love her. She's the daughter I lost in the war. You cannot understand what I've been through since I left her father. All these years, I've been thinking about how to keep my promise to Jonah. I helped him smuggle the girl out of the hell of the ghetto and must honor my covenant with him." Silence prevailed.

Pinchas tried to move the conversation forward. "Lazar greatly appreciates everything you've done for Elida, but the situation at the moment is that we need to start a legal procedure to allow her to live with him and Toibeh. They want to adopt her, but we will not do anything without your consent. The procedure is not simple. Lazar will give you money, which will compensate you for everything you've given her all these long years. He won't be able to do anything without your approval." Pinchas presented a document and explained, "Here's an agreement signed by a lawyer, and you'll be full partners in it."

Joel and Yocheved exchanged glances. Joel had been keeping a record of their expenses ever since they received Elida from Stanislava. He was ready to agree to the proposed financial settlement but knew how difficult it would be for Yocheved. If she has to say goodbye to Elida, it will be because of me, he thought. And she'll only agree because she wants a better future for the girl.

"We'd like some time to think about it," Joel said, softly this time.

Everyone agreed. "I just ask that you not wait too long

before giving your consent," Lazar said. "I need to return home to tend to my business, and we should get started on the many legal arrangements as soon as possible."

A few days later, Yocheved arrived at Leah's apartment in Haifa and announced, "We agree that Elida can travel to America." Lazar and Leah informed Elida that the Ruhin family had given their consent for her trip to America. They said this with relief and hoped that Elida would be happy to hear the news; they did not fully grasp Elida's vulnerability.

She turned her back on Lazar and Leah, walked out of the apartment, trudged down the stairs, and began roaming the streets of the neighborhood. Her heart sank like a stone in her chest, again.

Of course, they'll be happy to get rid of me, she thought. If they have to choose between me and money, they'll obviously choose money. It just shows what kind of parents they've been. Even Mame has given up on me. I'm not wanted anywhere. Leah also wants Lazar to take me; her children are more important to her. In Vilna, Mrs. Dinner told me that I had a family here that would love me. Some love! A girl who is passed from hand to hand. Lazar does pamper me, but mostly with money. I'll go with him because I have no choice. I've already said goodbye to Mame and Tate. Now I have to take care of myself. From now on, I'll do only what's good for me!

IN JULY 1957, THE FIRST ADOPTION HEARING WAS HELD IN Haifa District Court. The judge referred the case to the director of the Department of Social Work, requesting her assessment of Eliezer Goldberg's suitability for adopting Gita Ruhin. She had to check the sincerity of his intentions, verify the Ruhin couple's consent, and verify the girl's accord with the procedure.

Bella was not surprised when she received the case. She clearly remembered the immigrant couple and their daughter. At their meeting this time, Mrs. Ruhin looked tired and submissive. She did not utter a word against the girl's transfer to Mr. Goldberg.

"I know we have to give up the girl for her happiness. Our financial situation is difficult. The girl is particularly talented and deserves good schools. My husband's illness does not allow him to work. He is old and in a bad emotional state. I work hard in the laundry to support the family. We agreed to the adoption, even though it is very difficult for me to say goodbye to her."

Bella was shocked to learn that no official adoption procedure had been carried out in Lithuania by the Ruhin couple. In all the documents they presented when immigrating to Israel, Elida was listed as their daughter. But this was based solely on their own statements. It turned out that in Lithuania after the war, children who were hidden with Christian families and redeemed by Jews, as in the case of Elida, did not undergo an official adoption procedure.

In her meetings with Elida, Bella spoke Hebrew with her and admired her progress. When asked if it was difficult for her to part with the Ruhin family, Elida replied, "It was never a family. I suffered with them, and even in

Lithuania I wanted to leave them. I agreed to come to Israel because I knew that I had a family here. Since we arrived, I've been staying with my aunt, but I can't stay there forever. Lazar, who was closest to my real father, is very good to me and wants to give me a home and a family. I've become very attached to him. He'll be my family."

Bella was deeply impressed by her meeting with Mr. Goldberg, a pleasant-mannered man with warm blue eyes and a kind smile. She admired the fluent Hebrew he spoke. He told the story of his difficult life. When asked about his wife, he showered praise on her. "She is very interested, like me, in having Elida as our daughter. She experienced a lot of trouble during the war. She'll accept Elida as her daughter." Bella noted in the report that the adoptive father was trustworthy and kindhearted, but that further clarification was needed in regard to the prospective mother.

A memorandum in that spirit was forwarded to the court along with the recommendation to allow Mr. Goldberg to adopt Elida. In order for the adoption process to take place, his wife was asked to come to Israel in order to verify her suitability. In addition, the Department of Social Work requested an assessment of the Goldbergs from the welfare office in their city of residence.

The judge accepted these recommendations and froze the adoption process pending an assessment from the welfare authorities in Laredo, Texas, and an interview with Toibeh Goldberg in Israel. The judge also requested a written statement from the Ruhin family affirming that there was no official adoption procedure in Lithuania, and asked to meet with them to assess their willingness to hand over the girl.

Lazar was disappointed. He had hoped to take Elida with him, but now had to return home without her. His wife was looking after the business while he was in Israel and could only come to Israel to be interviewed when he returned. Lazar also feared that the longer Elida was in Israel, the harder it would be to detach her from her Israeli family.

The family kept Elida updated about the legal proceedings. "The court supports the adoption," she was told, "but they asked Toibeh to come to Israel, and she'll come after Lazar goes home. So that you'll have a chance to get to know her."

Her silence worried Lazar. The movement of her lips expressed mistrust. "Are you afraid I won't come back?" he asked. "I give you my promise. Toibeh will come, and she knows how to handle matters as well as I do, or even better. And in a few months, we'll be together permanently." Lazar's eyes watered as he said goodbye to her, but Elida stood motionless as he hugged her. She did not shed a tear or say a word. Lazar returned to America.

"How do you want to spend the day?" Leah asked Elida. "We can go to the sea, to the Carmel, or to the movies. It will cheer you up." Elida shook her head. "I will sit and read," she told Leah.

For two days, she refused any activity offered to her.

On the third day, she joined the family on an outing to the Bat Galim beach. On summer afternoons, the family would pack baskets and towels and take the bus to the beach. In her woolen swimsuit, Elida bathed in a natural pool created between the rocks. The caress of the water and the foam of the waves calmed her.

Lazar kept his promise. Light-blue envelopes arrived by airmail. He referred to her as "my dear daughter" in every letter. In one of the letters, he informed her that Toibeh was coming to Haifa in early September and would take care of all the arrangements required for Elida to come with her as their daughter to America. Elida agreed to visit Mame in Kiryat Haim only after receiving the letter about Toibeh's upcoming arrival. She wanted to be sure that Mame and Tate wouldn't tease her about being left behind by Lazar. Now she could tell Mame that Toibeh was coming and that her plan to travel to America would indeed materialize.

Elida still worried: What if the court decided that she must remain the Ruhins' daughter? When imagining this distressful scenario, she would start to concoct escape plans.

FINALLY, AT THE BEGINNING OF SEPTEMBER 1957, TOIBEH Goldberg arrived in Haifa and met Elida for the first time. Elida already knew her from the photographs she had seen but was distraught when she saw her in person. Before her stood a beautiful woman in a floral dress. She looked younger than all her aunts. This was not a mother, she thought, this was not how a mother should look; she was more like a Hollywood actress.

Elida's hands hung limply at her side as Toibeh hugged her and whispered to her, "*Mein kind.*" Yehudit, who witnessed this encounter, later reported to her sisters: "They have a long way to go before they become mother and daughter."

Toibeh spoke to Elida in Yiddish and treated her as Lazar had. She traveled with Elida alone or together with other children from the family. They went to have ice cream, to cafés on the Carmel or on Nordau Street, and met in the evenings with the aunts, chatting and telling stories. Toibeh was staying with Pinchas and Yehudit, and Elida with Leah. Two weeks later, things changed: Toibeh rented an apartment on Nordau Street and Elida and Toibeh moved in together. It was a hopeful time.

As the adoption dragged on, Elida remained ambivalent. She liked her new school, and the Hebrew language began to flow on her tongue. But she had not warmed to Toibeh the way she had with Lazar.

"Instead of understanding me, she's constantly trying to change me," she complained to her aunt Yaffa.

"Toibeh is a good woman," Yaffa replied. "She suffered greatly in the war. She only wants the best for you." Elida looked doubtful.

Elida tossed and turned in her bed at night. She heard Toibeh's sighs, as she, too, had a hard time falling asleep. Should I refuse to go to America even though they have done everything to make me their daughter? Lazar would be a good dad, the dad I never had, the closest to my real dad. After all, this is what I wanted, to have parents and a home, so what does it matter where, in America or in Israel?

When Elida was left alone in their apartment on Nordau Street, she opened the wardrobe on Toibeh's side and rummaged through her clothes. She spread out her floral blouses, examined the lilac-colored trousers, and stuck her nose between the hanging dresses. It reminded her of the smell of the packages that arrived in Vilna from America. She examined the large, clear bottles of soap, shampoo, and body lotion, smeared the ointments on her hands, and an unfamiliar and sweet scent arose from her body. Perhaps she, too, could in time assimilate into this wonderful world, like in the Doris Day movies she watched with her cousins.

Toibeh knew of Elida's love for American movies, and she told her about the house she would live in, about her room and her new furniture. "We have a car," she said, "and in another year you can drive it. We'll buy you some nice clothes and you'll have girlfriends there, cousins your age."

The law firm handling the adoption demanded a long list of documents in preparation for the district court hearing. In addition to the official adoption, Elida would need an American passport.

Toibeh wanted to go home. The temporary situation of the two living together with no official family status created tension. Under the guidance of the lawyers, Toibeh met with social workers from the Department of Social Work. She brought Elida to the meeting and occasionally put her arm around the girl's shoulder. The experienced social workers noticed that Elida fidgeted uncomfortably when Toibeh made any excessive gesture. Bella, who already knew Elida, noticed that despite her embarrassment, she was not angry as she had been with the Ruhin family, and her face was calmer. But the stark differences between the beautiful prospective mother and the tanned girl with the prominent chin could not be overlooked. The social workers asked Toibeh to come to another meeting without Elida and asked many questions about her past in order to examine her sincere willingness to adopt Gita Ruhin. Toibeh protested, "Why don't you call her Elida as she asks? She has already changed her name."

"That's the name that is still listed in the official documents," the social workers explained. "Court matters are conducted according to official documents."

The beautiful woman's confidence cracked when she began to recount her experiences during the war. She said that she had known Elida's parents in the ghetto and was a relative of Lazar's first wife, so she also knew him there. She was sent to Auschwitz and the Ravensbrück labor camp, escaped, and injured her leg. There was still a bullet in her leg that caused her a lot of pain. After the war, she returned to Kovno, hoping to find living relatives. That was how she met Lazar. They fled together and reached the DP camps in Italy, where they got married. They intended to travel to Israel, but the immigration certificates were delayed. They decided to take advantage of the permit sent from the United States by Lazar's brother, which allowed them to leave Europe. They maintained a traditional Zionist and Jewish home and dreamed of the day when they could live in Israel. Because of the suffering she experienced in the war, she could not give birth. When they learned that Elida had come to Israel, and that her relationship with her "parents" was not good and that she wanted to leave them, her husband immediately left the U.S. with the aim of adopting her, with her full consent.

One of the social workers probed Toibeh's attitude toward the Ruhin family. "It's true that they don't have any official document of adoption, but the girl has been their daughter for all intents and purposes since the end of the war."

"They have not been parents!" Toibeh burst out. "The father often beat her. Elida showed me scars on her body from the belt. She didn't receive from them what a child needs—warmth, love, security."

"And yet they gave her a home after the war. It was important to them to save a Jewish girl."

"Perhaps that's what the mother wanted, but not her husband. The war took away his every emotion, stole from him any possibility of raising children."

"Still, the mother is close to Gita. How did you convince them to give her up?"

"They understood that the girl wanted to be with her father's family. Things are difficult for the Ruhins; he doesn't earn a living and she works very hard. We promised that Elida would stay in touch with them. We come to Israel every year, and she'll come with us to visit them. Even now, even though she lives with me, we go together to Kiryat Haim, and Yocheved Ruhin has come to visit us in Haifa."

She's a smart woman, Bella thought to herself. She was well prepared for the meeting. A recommendation submitted by the social workers testified to the sincerity of the prospective mother and the Goldbergs' ability to give the girl a loving Jewish home. The recommendation was also accompanied by a report from a welfare inspector in Laredo, Texas, as requested by the court. The report complimented the Goldbergs and affirmed their ability to adopt the girl. The inspector testified that he had met both Lazar and Toibeh individually, visited their home and business, spoken with family members and others in the community, and was convinced of their ability to offer the girl a proper home and provide for all her needs.

"Mr. Lazar Goldberg," the report read, "has managed to build a successful business during his ten years in the United States. Their home is spacious, and tastefully and comfortably furnished. He is pleasant-mannered, intelligent, and an interesting conversationalist. He very generously helps and supports needy people; he connects easily, and people are happy around him." Toibeh Goldberg was described as a wise and warm woman involved in the Jewish community. "Her difficult life in the war has strengthened her. She knows how to appreciate the achievements they have made in building their new lives after the war. The fact that they are unable to have children and the possibility of adopting and accepting their family member as their daughter will make them very happy and the girl will be given a loving and warm home." The inspector also noted their awareness of the difficulties in adopting a fourteen-year-old girl who had grown up an orphan with burdens of loneliness and lack of love. "They will do everything to give her what was taken from her."

The fact that the Goldbergs were Jews and Zionists was important in the trial. Lazar Goldberg's Jewishness was unreservedly confirmed, but not Toibeh's. In order to approve the adoption of a Jewish girl, the rabbinical court demanded official confirmation that Toibeh and Elida were Jews. This was the most difficult task for Toibeh due to the personal insult involved.

"What's the problem, why are you insulted? You know that this is an official procedure. You have all the evidence to show that you are Jewish, and who will doubt that Elida is a Jew?" Yehudit, her sister-in-law, said to Toibeh. "I'll go with you and testify in court. I'm a family member, and I knew Tzila and your family. We all know that you are Jewish."

"I'm just angry that here in the Jewish state, after everything I went through, anyone dares to question my Jewishness. Do I need confirmation from the rabbis that I am Jewish?" Toibeh raised her voice.

"You're right," Yehudit agreed. "It's insulting, but there's no choice. Everything will work out."

Standing before the rabbinical court, she dressed modestly and wore a headscarf. The rabbis examined her American passport, which included both her married name, Goldberg, and her maiden name, Karnowski. Apart from the passport, she had no official documents. Where would Holocaust survivors obtain birth certificates? But significant evidence appeared on her forearm: the blue number of a death camp prisoner. She raised her arm in front of the judges and asked, "Do you want to know more about my Jewishness?" This, along with her fluent Yiddish and the Israeli relatives who came to testify on her behalf, convinced the rabbinical court.

The district court judge perused the file before him, read the report from the social workers recommending the adoption, and was impressed with the inspector's report from Texas. But something did not feel right. The parents who had raised Elida, who for ten years had regarded her as their daughter and came with her to Israel—what happened there? The court had requested an affidavit attesting to their waiver of the girl, and the affidavit was missing.

"What about the Ruhin couple's waiver?" the judge asked. "I am compelled to adjourn the hearing until the couple comes to court and testifies to the waiver."

The lawyer translated the judge's remarks to Toibeh. The expression of despair on Toibeh's face did not go unnoticed. She spoke passionately to the lawyer. "If there's another long postponement, we won't be able to get a passport for Elida. The American authorities won't issue a passport if we don't have an adoption permit. Ask the judge to hold the hearing tomorrow. I promise to bring the Ruhins here."

The lawyer turned to the judge and explained the urgency due to the procedure for issuing the passport at the U.S. consulate. "They have an affidavit from Mr. Joel Ruhin," he added.

"That's not enough," the judge snarled. "You know very well that I need the consent of both parents. Both of them must be brought before me. I can consider your request to hold the hearing tomorrow only if the Ruhins appear before me tomorrow."

Toibeh nodded her head. "Both will come," she confirmed.

The next day, the Ruhin couple appeared in court. In a fatherly tone, the judge leaned over the podium and in a soft voice asked them if they were willing to transfer their daughter, Gita Ruhin, for adoption to Eliezer and Toibeh Goldberg from Texas. His voice radiated empathy toward them. They were properly dressed for a court appearance, but their clothes—Joel in an old suit and Yocheved in an unfashionable black dress—betrayed their condition. In the eyes of the judge, the contrast between Yocheved's gray figure and Toibeh's young and fresh appearance was apparent. He asked more than once to understand the reason for their willingness to hand over the girl to the Goldbergs.

Yocheved, in a quiet and firm voice, told their story—how they had come to Lithuania as refugees from Russia and redeemed the girl from Stanislava, giving her a new name: Gita Ruhin. She testified that no official procedure was carried out and that there were no formal papers. "Your Honor, it was after the war. There were no courts. It was total chaos. We filled out papers and Gita was listed everywhere as our child. Those were her credentials. We wanted to come to Israel, and we already knew that the girl might be adopted by her biological family. It's hard here in Israel. My husband is older than me, and he's sick and cannot make a living. I go to work every day to support us. We cannot provide the education needed for a smart and intelligent girl. We are releasing her, knowing that the Goldbergs can give her a home with many more opportunities."

Yocheved's testimony, in a mix of Yiddish and a little Hebrew, was recorded in the protocol. When Yocheved stepped down from the podium, Toibeh took her hand, embraced her, and whispered to her in Yiddish, "Thank you, thank you." The judge issued his decision later that day, approving the adoption.

The day after the adoption was approved, a meeting was scheduled for Toibeh with the lawyer who was handling the official documents for obtaining an American passport.

"We have to contend with another obstacle," the lawyer informed her. "The problem is not with the adoption permit you received, but with the birth of Elida in Kovno, Lithuania. The United States has quotas for the number of Lithuanian immigrants allowed to enter. The fact that Elida is already in Israel doesn't solve the problem. The immigration authorities cannot ignore the place of birth of passport applicants. All my attempts to convince the consul failed. 'A rule is a rule!' the consul insisted."

The erudite and matter-of-fact lawyer was not indifferent to Toibeh's sighs and the pallor of her face. As he reached out to place his hand on her arm, he noticed her instinctive movement to hide the number on it. "Despair is not an acceptable option," he told her. "We'll find a way to get the passport. Give me a day or two."

In the afternoon, Toibeh returned to the apartment, dragging herself with difficulty. Elida immediately felt her silence. Toibeh's face had beamed with joy upon receiving the adoption permit but was now shadowed in sadness. Elida insisted that she tell her what was going on, but Toibeh replied briefly, "Plane tickets are being arranged and now I have to lie down because I have a bad headache, my migraine."

The door of Toibeh's room slammed shut, and this was a signal for Elida to go and find out what was going on. She went to ask Pinchas why the trip to America was not working out. Pinchas sighed when he saw her enter the store, and this did not go unnoticed. "Truth is the best excuse," he always used to say. So he decided to tell her about the immigration obstacle. "It's nobody's fault. These are America's laws. However, we have a good lawyer, and he'll find a way to solve the problem."

"And what if he doesn't? I won't return to Kiryat Haim!" Her mouth became a thin crack and her hands clenched into fists. Pinchas was already acquainted with this reaction.

"I promise you everything will work out!"

The lawyer did not give up. He turned to a colleague who worked in the United States and asked him to urgently send him the immigration regulations pertaining to children. On the phone, the lawyer informed him of the latest regulations, issued only recently, in August 1957. It turned out that the quota restriction did not apply to children under the age of fourteen. The obstacle now facing them was Elida's recorded date of birth. Her birthday, which appeared on the birth certificate and in the registration documents upon her immigration to Israel, was November 10, 1942. According to this date, Elida would be fifteen years old in three weeks. The lawyer summoned Toibeh to an urgent meeting and immediately began to interrogate her: "What is Elida's exact age? Is it possible that the age listed on her certificates is inaccurate? Are there original certificates proving when she was born?"

"What original certificates?" Toibeh grinned bitterly. "Do you think anyone in the ghetto recorded the birth? You know it was forbidden to give birth! She was born in the ghetto! Only the family knew about her birth." Her voice was spiced with anger and insult at the very question, and then bewilderment at the contented smile that spread across the lawyer's face.

"That is our solution!" he exclaimed. "We need to find witnesses who can confirm that Elida was born in early 1944. Such proof will help us change her age. Then, she'll only be fourteen in January 1958 and will be able to enter the United States."

"How can we prove that? My husband was there when she was born, but his testimony won't be accepted."

"Think carefully, who can still testify about the date of birth? Any acquaintances? Perhaps a doctor from the hospital?"

"Hospital? You have no idea what kind of hell it was there. Who gave birth in a hospital? In spite of everything, Elida's mother decided to give birth to a child—but it had to be in hiding, in the dark." Toibeh suddenly fell silent. A spark appeared in her eyes, and she said happily, "Dr. Aharon Peretz! He lives here in Haifa. He assisted at her birth, and he can testify! He was a friend of Jonah's. They had worked together in the ghetto hospital, and he's also my husband's friend."

"If we weren't meeting in a professional setting, I would kiss you!" the lawyer exclaimed.

IN THE AFTERNOON, ELIDA NOTICED AN IMPROVEMENT IN Toibeh's mood. "Let's go to a café here on Nordau Street," Toibeh suggested.

While enjoying their ice cream, cake, and coffee, Toibeh explained to Elida why she had been so tense and what solution they had found. Elida peppered Toibeh with questions: "So, I'm not going to be fifteen? When was I born? Will Dr. Peretz agree to testify?" She remembered visiting him with Lazar, and that he had told her how much she resembled her father. "I'm older than fourteen," she added. "I know that."

"The time will come when you'll want to be younger. That's how it is with women," Toibeh said. "Do you think I'm the age listed on my passport? I'm younger too!"

"So, what do we do now? What will the lawyer do?"

"He's looking into it now," Toibeh replied, examining Elida's face. When will I get to see her pleased and smiling? she wondered. "Our lawyer is excellent and assured us that everything will work out. He'll talk to Dr. Peretz and arrange for him to testify."

"And what if Dr. Peretz is unwilling to testify about my date of birth?"

"I'm sure he'll agree to testify. He remembers when you were born because he assisted in delivering you. He won't say anything wrong." Toibeh was sorry she had shared this with Elida prematurely, but she did believe everything would work out and had wanted to make her happy. But now she realized that Elida should be told things only when they were certain to occur.

Time was pressing. The lawyer confirmed the court's requirements for issuing a declaratory order to officially change Elida's age. They would need the testimony of the doctor who witnessed her birth in the ghetto and an X-ray of Elida's hand, which would provide an approximate indication of the girl's biological age. All involved mobilized to expedite the process of confirming Elida's date of birth.

On the last day of October 1957, two weeks after the adoption order was issued, the Haifa District Court ruled that after reviewing the application and statements, especially in light of Dr. Peretz's testimony that Elida was born in early 1944, the date of birth listed on her Israeli passport could be amended accordingly. All her other official documents were also quickly amended after she was registered in the Israeli Population Registry as Elida Goldberg, daughter of Eliezer and Toibeh Goldberg, who was born in January 1944 in Kovno, Lithuania, and immigrated to Israel in April 1957. The road to her new home in America was now open.

ELIDA'S LAST TWO WEEKS IN ISRAEL WERE FULL OF BOTH joy and anxiety. She imagined herself on a busy street, with tall buildings and many people around her speaking English, of which she understood nothing. She repeatedly examined herself in the mirror, her curly brown hair, her aquiline nose, and her prominent chin. This was not how American girls looked. Where would her school be? How would she read books? In Israel, everyone speaks Yiddish and people also know Russian and Lithuanian. In Israel, people know where she came from, but there?

She also felt sorry for Mame. How hard it would be for Mame in Israel without her. All she had left was to take care of Tate.

On the last day before the flight, Elida went to Kiryat Haim to say goodbye to Mame and Tate. When she arrived, a pale-faced Tate sat at the table with the eternal cup of tea in front of him. He asked questions about the flight and where she would live and what she knew about the school she would go to. "I trust you to be a good student there and that the education you received from us will help you there in the new land." He did not kiss her when she left but extended his bony hand and stroked her hair.

Mame accompanied her outside with a brown bag in her hands. "I put your pictures and ours in it, pictures from your childhood and pictures with friends from Vilna."

Elida took the package and said nothing. They hugged again and again. Elida smelled the familiar smell of cooking and tasted the salty tears flowing, both hers and Mame's. Mame hugged her again and murmured "*mein kind.*"

That night she opened the bag. There were photographs of her with her girlfriends and the picture of her as a little girl with cropped black hair hugging a woman with blond braids and another girl on the other side, also blond. A warm wave flooded her. There was also a picture she knew well—a picture from which she had cut out the figures of Tate and Mame and left only herself. She remembered the day she had cut the picture and was ashamed. She decided not to destroy it but to bury it deep at the bottom of a drawer that would be only hers in her new home. There were also diplomas from school and her certificates of excellence.

That evening, the whole family gathered to say goodbye to Elida and Toibeh. The aunts baked cakes, cups of tea were served to the adults, and the children gathered in the other room and chatted.

Leah asked to speak to Elida privately. She hugged her

and said she was sorry that Elida had not become her daughter. "But you'll always be like a daughter to me. You're my brother's daughter and I love you. When you grow up, you'll surely understand our difficulties and the power of the promise your father and Lazar made to each other. The power of this promise, and the love and possibilities Lazar will give you, will help you live a good and happy life.

"I know we'll see each other many more times," Leah told her. "You'll visit us every year. We'll write letters and stay in touch." Elida did not protest or comment. She looked into her aunt's eyes and nodded, her mouth shrinking into a gesture of a smile, a smile of acceptance.

The next morning, Friday, December 20, 1957, Elida and Toibeh flew to America. Eight months after arriving in Israel as Gita, the daughter of Joel and Yocheved Ruhin, she arrived in the United States as Elida, the daughter of Lazar and Toibeh Goldberg.

5

Elida Goldberg, United States

THE ADDRESS TOIBEH GAVE THE CABDRIVER was in the southern part of Manhattan. They settled into a small hotel. Toibeh explained to Elida that she had chosen the hotel because it was located near Abrasha and Reizele Dinner's apartment. "They are our partners in the textile business. I have to take advantage of the fact that I'm in New York to do some work." This was the first Elida had heard about Abrasha, Leike Dinner's brother, who had survived the ghetto.

But Elida wasn't listening. She kept gazing at the tall buildings. She had to tilt her head back more and more to see their tops. In the streets, she saw more people than she had ever seen before. Some wore rags, while there were also men in elegant dark suits and coats, wearing hats.

Lazar also arrived in New York. He hugged and kissed

Elida and kept calling her "*mein kind.*" As in Haifa, he led her by the hand into lavish stores, and he offered to buy her whatever she wanted.

The meeting with Abrasha and his wife was similar to meetings with family members in Haifa. They hugged her, shed tears, noted how much she resembled Jonah, and burst into tears again.

In a letter to Leike in Vilna, she wrote, "For the family, I'm a memory of the war and of the ghetto. I'm a symbol of what happened to my father and to them. I want to be someone else."

Leike wrote to Lazar:

> *Accept the girl as she is. The past oppresses her, and she cannot carry the burden of our tragic history on her shoulders. She has experienced enough trouble and upheavals. We need to spare her the painful stories.*

AUNT LEAH WAS THE ONE WHO SUGGESTED "FIXING" ELIDA'S face or changing her prominent chin with plastic surgery. As soon as they arrived in New York, Toibeh arranged a consultation with a plastic surgeon. At an elegant clinic on Fifth Avenue, the doctor examined the new patient. A mother and her daughter, it said in the documents before him. The blond woman with perfect facial structure was not the biological mother of the girl with the prominent chin, the doctor concluded. At first he spoke English, but then switched to Yiddish.

The doctor held Elida's face between his fingers, turned it right and left, felt her chin, and mumbled obscure syllables. Elida blushed. Her face burned. She did not like her appearance, but Toibeh's haste to change it and the doctor's apparent concurrence that her face needed "fixing" made her feel humiliated and rejected. He scribbled a sketch on a piece of paper and explained what could be done.

AFTER TEN DAYS IN NEW YORK, THE FAMILY FLEW TO Texas. In San Antonio, Moy Goldberg, the family's adult nephew, was waiting for them in a Buick to drive them home to Laredo. The difference between New York and Texas stunned Elida. She hunched in the corner of the back seat and stared at the desert landscape passing before her eyes. The road stretched in a straight line to the horizon and retreated further and further. It was almost empty of cars. Occasionally, Moy increased his speed and passed a truck or van carrying cows or horses huddled together.

Lazar and Moy spoke English. Lazar's accent was so prominent that it sounded to her as if he were speaking Yiddish, but she still did not understand their conversation. A sense of alienation gripped her again. She noticed Moy staring at her through the rearview mirror. He looked at her curiously. "Moy is my brother Samuel's son, he's your cousin. He's a lawyer!" Lazar boasted. Elida did not respond and sat in silence. The heat, the desert around them, and the silence in the car overwhelmed her. Toibeh seemed to read her mind.

"New York is not America," she said. "America is great, and it has places of all kinds," she added.

"I see," Elida replied dryly, shrinking even further in the seat.

"Look, look!" Toibeh shook her excitedly. "We've arrived! This is Laredo!" They entered a flat town, with no forest or grove. Elida sat frozen by the window and watched the streets and wooden huts where dark-skinned women stood with a child or two in their arms and several other children were playing in the sand or riding a donkey, frolicking in an incomprehensible language.

"These are the Mexicans," Lazar explained to Elida. "These are their neighborhoods. We live in a beautiful big house." The car meandered through the streets and came to a wide street with houses surrounded by greenery and spacious lawns.

"You see, this is our street," Lazar said. The car slowed down and stopped near a green-painted wooden house.

"We're home at last. Welcome!" Lazar encouraged Elida. Toibeh was silent. After accompanying Elida for the last few months, she was accustomed to the unexpected moods of the girl who was now her daughter. She knew full well that even Lazar's excitement wouldn't necessarily make Elida cheerful.

Maria, the devoted Mexican maid, stood on the staircase leading to the house and waved her hands enthusiastically. When she saw Toibeh, she ran toward her and hugged her. Then, after receiving permission, she ran and spread her arms to greet the new girl.

Elida looked at her suspiciously. During the time she had spent in New York, she had gotten used to colorful figures, but the personal closeness that Maria displayed bothered her.

Toibeh and Lazar's house was located on Mayer Street. It was no different from the rest of the houses on the street—wooden houses painted white or beige and even green like her new house. A number of steps led to a porch and a doorway that invited visitors inside. In the center of the house, there was a kitchen with accessories that Elida had never seen before. An oversized electric refrigerator, a wide oven, a mixer, and an electric coffee machine. There were three bedrooms and a bathroom. The house was clean and furnished with an impressive dining table, armchairs, and a broad sofa. The room designated for Elida had been prepared for her arrival. A wide bed, a wardrobe, and even a desk—a piece of furniture she had so far only seen in libraries—and empty bookshelves. A white wicker armchair stood in the corner.

If they would just let her get into the inviting bed and sleep endlessly, she thought. She was confused, choked with a longing for something undefined.

Elida wanted to be left alone and for everyone to stop trying to squeeze joy out of her. They were waiting to hear her say how great it was and how they had saved her, but she could not feel happy. She was anxious about the future.

Soon they called her again. "Here's my brother Raoul," Lazar bellowed, introducing a smiling man with blue eyes. "And this is his wife, Angelina." They smiled at her and reached out to shake her hand. There was something delicate and warm in their gaze. "They have five children," Lazar declared. "They are your family." Samuel, Moy's father, also came with his wife, Mania, and they, too, congratulated her on her arrival.

As in Haifa, Elida constructed a protective wall around herself. The family in Haifa had also been excited at first, but then passed her on. What if she were at a temporary station again, and from here they'd move her to another place? She needed an escape route, she thought. And then she noticed a door that led from the dining room to the backyard, to the green grass. She slipped into the yard and walked back and forth. Suddenly, she felt eyes fixed on her. At the window of the house stood a boy, one of Raoul's children, watching her. He raised his hand and waved at her. She gave him a small smile. There was something nice about him, familiar. She looked away. Inside the house, the family rejoiced, but Elida was left alone in the yard.

NEW STRUGGLES BEGAN IMMEDIATELY. LAZAR WANTED Elida to call him "Daddy" and his wife "Mommy," but Elida refused. They were Toibeh and Lazar to her. Lazar took her everywhere and proudly introduced her to his every acquaintance: "This is our daughter!" He solemnly entered his store on Convent Street and presented her to his employees. Lazar was proud of his business. He had arrived in America as a war refugee just ten years ago, and here he was, a respected and well-liked merchant with a textile store full of beautiful fabrics.

Now that the Christmas holidays were over and schools were reopening, Lazar and Toibeh needed to find a place for Elida. Most public schools would not admit a girl who didn't speak English, and in the middle of the year, no less. The best option turned out to be a private Catholic school, Ursuline Academy, whose teaching staff included nuns wearing black habits with white collars.

The campus was not far from Elida's new home. Among the impressive classroom buildings was a large courtyard surrounded by manicured gardens. The school was for girls only. The students wore a uniform that included a skirt, a blouse, and knee-high white socks.

When Elida first entered the new school, she felt happy. On the picture-laden walls, she saw a mother holding her baby son, who was adorned with a halo over his head. The smell of incense rose from one of the rooms, and she felt she had reached a familiar place. She was ushered into a classroom, and a teacher, a smiling young nun, greeted her. There were several girls in the class, all of them immigrants. Here she would learn English.

The school gave her confidence. From the start, the

English teacher noticed the new student's aptitude and broad education and encouraged her. Order and discipline suited her. Something here reminded her of the school she missed in Vilna. At the school in Israel, she had been surrounded by noise and commotion, Hebrew-speaking boys and girls who radiated self-confidence. And here she was again learning a new language. Would she ever read books in English like she read in Russian, books that filled her world?

In the evenings before bed, she wandered among the words she had acquired. She often translated from English into Russian and vice versa. She lit the bedside lamp—a wondrous item to her—and read a book the teacher had given her to practice her English. Every day, she absorbed new words and expressions from her school lessons and from the books she began to borrow from the school library. She soon realized that she should put aside the books in Russian she had brought with her and get acquainted with English literature.

She acknowledged to herself that the evenings in her room and the hours she spent at school were good for her. The difficulties were with her parents, whom she repeatedly tested to see how firm their decision was to adopt her.

Toibeh and Lazar, for their part, overlooked her silence and her refusal to call them Mommy and Daddy. She insisted on talking to them in English rather than Yiddish, and they suffered through her tantrums. And still they tried.

To bolster her knowledge of the new language, they arranged private lessons by a young schoolteacher who taught English language and literature. Her name was Virginia Kazen. Three times a week Elida went to the Kazen residence, an elegant house not far from their home. The Kazens were one of the most esteemed families in Laredo. The father was a Catholic of Lebanese descent, a lawyer who had recently been appointed a district judge. The family had three daughters. Virginia was the eldest. The first time Elida came to their house, she was excited. The furniture in the house was made of mahogany, the walls were covered with pictures, and heavy curtains hung beside the large windows. Virginia brought her into their library, and it took her breath away. All the walls were covered with shelves laden with books. Rows and rows of thick and thin books. She looked at them with longing. Virginia caught her eye. "Soon you'll be able to read as many books as you want," she told her. Tears welled up in Elida's eyes.

"Let's get started," Virginia suggested, pulling a book off a shelf. "We'll read *Uncle Tom's Cabin,* but before we get started, please tell me a little about yourself in the English you already know."

Elida pursed her lips. "I don't have much to tell," she replied. "I came from Vilna and studied in a school where Russian was the language. I really like books and have read many books in Russian. The most important thing for me is to know how to read books in English, because there are no books in Russian here."

Virginia realized very quickly that Elida would not open up to her about her previous life. They spent more than a year reading and talking together, but Elida resisted any attempt by Virginia to touch upon her past or share her feelings. Classes with Virginia were the happiest hours for Elida, and Virginia was full of admiration for her. None of the girls Elida's age resembled her. "The girl is uniquely smart and talented," Virginia told her parents. "Her ability to absorb the language amazes me."

But Elida was not content with just studying at her teacher's home. The Kazen family residence soon became a second home for her. She befriended the other two Kazen girls, stayed after classes, and asked to come to their home almost daily. Aside from their rich library, she loved the family dinners, to which she was often invited. Everyone sat around the table politely, and the conversations the girls had with their parents revolved around politics, the books the girls read, and their feelings. How much she wanted to belong to a family like this one, free of painful history! There were evenings after dinner when the whole family would sit around the table quietly listening to albums of classical music. The girls in the family played the piano, and the youngest played the violin. Elida had learned to play the piano and violin at the conservatory in Vilna, but she had not touched a musical instrument for two years. Still, she agreed to play the instruments for the Kazens and their applause pleased her.

The close connection with the Kazen family flattered Toibeh and Lazar at first, and they appreciated how much the Kazens cared for Elida. But as time passed and the bond grew stronger, they became jealous. They started insisting that Elida come home for dinner.

This sudden demand made Elida angry. "I cannot talk to you about a book we've read. Your language is Yiddish. Have you noticed that you speak Yiddish with me? For you, I'm the past, not the future. You live in your narrow world, and I want to live in another world."

After such outbursts, Lazar's eyes would fill with tears, and Toibeh would slam her fist on the table and fire at Elida, "You're ungrateful!"

"What are you lacking?" Lazar would rush to appease Elida. "What do you want us to buy, a piano? We'll buy a piano! Just tell us what you want."

As always, Toibeh left the kitchen angrily and shot at him, "You just pamper her. She needs to be disciplined! She should respect us, not just receive more and more gifts."

After three months, Elida was transferred to a regular class. Her academic excellence in all subjects immediately stood out. The nuns who taught her admired her abilities. "Her knowledge is outstanding," Toibeh and Lazar were informed. "She is the most mature of all the girls in her class."

The Goldbergs understood that Elida's adjustment to her new parents and to such a different world would be hard for the teenager, but they longed for a peaceful and idyllic family.

Toibeh believed that the first step to easing her new

daughter's integration would be a change in her image. And so Toibeh, her aunts, and her cousins, Thelma and Martha, taught her how to pluck her eyebrows and shave her armpits, and they showed her what types of shampoos and hair curlers to use for straightening her frizzy hair and wearing it up with a ribbon. New clothes filled her closet. "We need to emphasize your beautiful legs," Toibeh told her. "Shorts with a colorful blouse will suit you.

"Why is she upset with me when I buy her a lot of clothes and make sure she looks like all the girls her age?" Toibeh complained to her sisters-in-law.

"Maybe you shouldn't give her so much at once," Angelina told her.

Elida found in Angelina an attentive ear and a warm and wise soul with whom she could share some of her secrets. Just a week earlier, Elida had complained to Angelina that she felt like a windup doll, with the key turned so it would cry or laugh, raise its hands or walk. "They ask me to do whatever they think is right for me and they don't ask what I want," she told her. Angelina refrained from conveying that exact message to Toibeh for fear of upsetting her.

"It's not about new clothes and hair," she told Toibeh, "it's about changing what she feels inside."

At night, Elida thought of Mame. In a letter, she wrote:

Dear Mame, I hope everything is fine with you, that you are healthy and that you are not working too hard. My new world is good to me. I really like my school. I already speak English and also know how to read and write in that language, although I still have a lot to learn. We're arranging a package for you. Do not be ashamed to write what you need most. I think about you a lot.

In her first letters, she refrained from mentioning her name. What should she write, Elida Goldberg? Or go back to being Gita again?

When she thought back on Vilna, she was amazed at how much affection she felt. In a conversation with Virginia about the meaning of the term "nostalgia," Virginia helped her understand her longing. "The past has a great presence because of what you lost in it," Virginia told her. "You lost your childhood."

Elida's new family often had their picture taken. The photos were sent to relatives in Israel in the weekly envelope with the letters describing Elida's integration. The Ruhin family also received photos occasionally.

TO LIVE IN LAREDO AS A DAUGHTER OF THE GOLDBERG family meant to belong to the local Jewish community. The Goldberg brothers helped arrange for prayers in the synagogue, recruited a rabbi, donated to Jewish charities, and held fundraising events for the State of Israel. Oil paintings of Jerusalem and a picture of a bearded Jew with a black hat hung in their house. A silver menorah stood in a display case in the living room, and also silver candlesticks that Toibeh used on Friday nights.

Lazar would have liked Elida to join him as an observant Jew, but she refused to accompany him when he went to synagogue on Fridays and Saturdays. Jewish rituals unnerved her. When Lazar greeted her with "*shabbat shalom*" on the Jewish sabbath or when the extended Goldberg family gathered around the festive table on Passover, she felt detached. She had a sense of alienation when it came to her Judaism, but she did not discuss it with anyone, not even with Virginia.

Being part of the extended Goldberg family also meant interacting with her cousins Thelma, Martha, Havale, and Moy. Elida spent most Sundays with her female cousins, and sometimes they would go to the movies together. After Elida's appearance was redesigned and she wore the same clothes as the others, she looked like them but inside she still felt remote. Her English was fluent, but in a photograph of the cousins from that period, she sat with slumped shoulders, a forced smile, and a veiled look.

Once Elida arrived at Lazar's home, the past was erased. No one talked about her previous life. To her cousins, she was the daughter of Lazar and Toibeh and that was it. She was comfortable with the forgetting.

"IN THE SUMMER, WE'LL GO TO NEW YORK, TO THE DOCTOR we saw, and have the surgery, and then you'll see how beautiful you'll be." Toibeh would occasionally repeat this sentence, referring to the visit to the plastic surgeon, a visit that Elida had found so humiliating.

"I don't want surgery," Elida would tell Toibeh. "I want to stay the way I am!"

Toibeh was angry. "We've talked about it many times. You should be glad we can afford it!"

After this conversation, Toibeh stopped mentioning the operation to Elida but still set a date with the surgeon in New York. She decided to let Lazar tell her; he knew how to soften Elida's heart. One evening, when they were both alone at home, he complimented her on her academic success and then said: "*Mein kind*, you know that I love you and want the best for you. And I'm also fortunate to have the money to provide it. That includes taking you to the best surgeon in New York. Just as some children need braces so that their teeth don't protrude, you can have surgery so that your jaw doesn't protrude. If you agree, I'll plan the trip to New York. But only if you agree."

"We'll see," Elida said.

That night she couldn't fall asleep. She got out of bed, stood in front of the mirror, and examined her face, moving it left and right. They're right, she thought, something has to be done about this face. She could not ignore how people looked at her chin.

And so, Elida consented and Toibeh began preparations for a trip to New York.

In New York, they stayed at the same hotel as before. Elida again felt excited by the bustling metropolis. At the doctor's office, Elida was interested in his drawings, asked questions, and stood up to be photographed from different angles. Toibeh sat on the side and did not intervene.

The operation was performed. Bandaged and sore, Elida shut herself in the hotel, reading nonstop the books Virginia had sent with her. "She's been reading books in English from cover to cover," Toibeh boasted to her acquaintances. It was two weeks before it was possible to leave the room without a bandage, and even then, there were bruises on her face, blue, yellow, and black. The doctor promised that they would disappear, and he was proud of the work he had done. Elida stood in front of the mirror and examined herself. Her chin was wider and did not protrude anymore, her lips were rounded, and her nose was less prominent, but she had difficulty expressing her satisfaction.

"If she's not angry with me and doesn't blame me, I'm satisfied," Toibeh wrote to Angelina.

Elida was pleased to return to Laredo at the end of the summer break. She missed her school and English classes, her friends' homes, the Kazen family, and the books in their library.

As soon as they returned to Laredo, members of the extended Goldberg family gathered for a reception, curious to see the change in Elida's appearance. Cries of admiration were heard from everyone. "Can't believe what can be done today," the adults chirped, while the young people, especially the girls, circled around her and examined her. Havale said, "You're very beautiful now." Elida smiled awkwardly.

•

ELIDA HAPPILY WALKED TO SCHOOL EVERY MORNING. She loved school and the teachers loved her. They appreciated her wisdom, her vast knowledge, the good English she spoke. She'd only been there a year and was already reading serious books. The nuns at the school smiled pleasantly when they spoke to her. They took good care of her, and she was grateful.

But Toibeh felt that Elida was drifting away from them. Her long stays at the Kazen residence continued to rankle her: "She has dinner with them and comes to us just to sleep." However, when Lazar and Toibeh were invited with Elida to the Kazen family home for Christmas dinner, Toibeh regarded it as a great honor.

"Jews don't celebrate Christmas," Lazar objected.

"It's a great honor for us that such a respectable family invites us. They have no ulterior motives."

"And what if they serve us nonkosher food?"

Elida urged them to accept the invitation, but as the time approached, she started getting nervous and began instructing Lazar and Toibeh on how to behave, what to say, and what to avoid. She promised them that the meal would not include any nonkosher food.

"I don't owe them anything," Lazar grumbled.

"But now that we've already agreed, it's too late to cancel," Toibeh concluded.

On the eve of the holiday, they arrived at the Kazen

residence in their best attire. The table was tastefully set. The conversation around the table revolved around the meaning of the holiday, politics, and a book that Virginia had read. Toibeh and Lazar did not participate much. Envious, Toibeh watched how Elida fit into the conversation and how the family members nodded as she voiced her opinion. That night, as they lay in their beds, Elida heard Toibeh and Lazar whispering. It was late. "It's going to end badly, this relationship," Lazar argued. "Maybe we were wrong to send her to that school."

"That's nonsense," Toibeh replied. "She loves the school, is loved there and successful. It's still considered the best school in the area."

Elida shuddered. If they try to transfer me to another school, I'll fight, she thought. It's best for me there; why should I go to an inferior public school? They always think I can be moved from one place to another as they wish.

The light in their room went out and the talking stopped, but Elida continued to toss restlessly in her bed. In her mind, she devised plans in case she had to fight for her right to continue attending her school.

ELIDA FOUND A SENSE OF CALMNESS AT SCHOOL. THE NUNS, whose habits reached the floor, seemed to float. Sister Anna gently placed her hand on Elida's shoulder when she saw her. To her, Anna resembled the Holy Mother, who looked at her from every picture on the school walls. Elida usually passed by the prayer room, but one day she decided to go in. She sat on one of the outer benches arranged in a semicircle and watched the flickering candles and a statue of Mary embracing Jesus. The experience moved her.

A secret began to form within her. She talked at length with Anna, whispering her secret: "I want to convert to Christianity." Anna instructed her to think carefully before deciding about this step.

Elida slipped out of school, saying she had a headache. She went home and locked herself in her room. She knew it would upset Lazar, but she believed that becoming a Christian would finally free her from the anguish of the past. She could become someone new. Lazar and Toibeh noticed that their daughter was in turmoil. She was angry about everything.

Then one morning, as her parents were at the breakfast table, Elida entered the kitchen and instead of saying good morning, she announced to Toibeh and Lazar: "I intend to convert to Christianity!"

Toibeh's cup of coffee dropped from her hand and shattered on the floor. Lazar got up and, in a voice he had never used before, shouted, "What did you say? Tell me that I did not understand you!"

Elida repeated the sentence. "I'm converting!"

Lazar approached her and slapped her face. His face was flushed. "Over my dead body!" he shouted. "You will not do anything of the sort. After everything we went through, what your father went through, how could you even dare to think about it?!"

Toibeh sat in silence for a while and then suddenly stood and shouted, "Out! Not in our house!"

"I'm not asking for your permission. I know what's good for me," Elida stubbornly replied. With tears streaming down her cheeks, she slammed the door and left the house. She lingered a little in the yard and then ran to Angelina's house, because Angelina was the only one she could talk to about her troubles. She walked into the kitchen, where Angelina was sitting with her eternal cigarette and a cup of coffee. When she saw Elida, she smiled at her and invited her to sit down. Angelina saw Elida's teary face and knew she was about to hear another story about a quarrel.

Elida blurted it out. "I want to convert to Christianity, and I've just informed Toibeh and Lazar of my decision."

"You cannot do that!" Angelina raged. "Do you want to kill Lazar? No, you will not convert to Christianity! Your family has turned the world upside down to keep you and bring you to a Jewish family, who went through hell because they are Jews. Your father requested that you grow up as a Jew. I won't support you! More than that, I'll stand against you. A girl does not make such a decision alone. Who put this idea in your head, the nuns at school?"

Elida hung her head. She had thought that Angelina would protect her, but here, too, she was rejected.

At the sound of their mother's loud voice, Moy and Thelma came to the kitchen and saw that Elida had been crying.

"What happened?" Moy asked. Elida did not answer.

"Did something happen to Uncle Lazar?" he probed.

"Yes," she replied. "Me."

THE FAMILY WENT INTO OVERDRIVE. TOIBEH WENT TO speak with Mrs. Kazen and sat with her for several hours, telling the story of her survival in the Holocaust, Lazar's story, and of course Elida's story. Mrs. Kazen held Toibeh's hand and could not stop crying. She assured her that she did not know about Elida's intention to convert and was also sure that the teachers at the school had not proselytized her.

The next day, Lazar drove to San Antonio. He enlisted the help of his nephew, a lawyer, who introduced him to a local Catholic public figure, who was also a lawyer. Lazar told him Elida's story, shared his feelings, and asked for help from the Catholic religious leadership. He also asked whether the law could prevent the conversion of a sixteen-year-old girl against the will of her parents. The possibility of banning Elida from returning to Catholic school also came up. Those were difficult days for everyone.

The lawyer contacted the school principal, who assured him that none of the nuns had persuaded or encouraged Elida to become a Christian. Toibeh and Lazar met with the principal and two of her teachers, who apologized and insisted that it had never occurred to them that Elida's studies at their school would make her want to convert to Christianity. They asked that the Goldbergs allow her to continue at the school and vowed to keep her away from religious classes and prayers. She was a very special student, they said, and it would be a shame to remove her from her beloved school and transfer her to another setting that might not suit her talents. They also discussed allowing Elida to skip a year and join the senior class.

During the meeting, Lazar remained steadfast. "I will not allow even a small chance that my daughter reject Judaism. We need to think about whether she should stay on at this school."

There were more consultations, with arguments for and against, and meanwhile Elida shut herself in her room with her books and remained silent. She did not go into the kitchen to eat with her parents or show up for the piano lessons she had begun to take that year. She felt the space that had opened up in her heart was shrinking again.

I will never, ever be able to be myself, she thought to herself. I will never be able to feel liberated.

About two weeks after the storm erupted, Toibeh and Lazar called her to sit and talk with them. "If you promise to never again raise this idea of converting, we'll let you continue at your school. We've spoken to the principal and your teachers, and they've assured us that the school will be a place for your studies only! Any contact with religion will end. But only if we have your promise can we allow you to continue."

Elida was silent for a few minutes. Her parents were silent too. Finally, she said: "I will not convert." She raised her head toward Lazar and saw glistening tears in his eyes. He leaned over and kissed her on the cheek, as did Toibeh. Then they ate their dinner in silence.

TOWARD THE END OF THE SCHOOL YEAR, HER VISITS TO the Kazen family became less frequent. Virginia was about to get married and move to another city.

In the summer, during family reunions on Sundays, Elida got closer to her cousins and especially to Thelma and Martha. She already spoke English fluently, and she also mastered Spanish and conversed with the local Mexicans. Among the photos that reached family members in Israel, Elida was seen wearing jeans and a denim jacket, her hands in her pockets, and she was smiling. On the photo she wrote: "Hurray for Texas! Love, Elida."

A year later, Elida was placed in an advanced class, as agreed.

LIFE WENT ON. LAZAR AND TOIBEH'S BUSINESS PROSPERED, and they purchased a spacious house with a pool in the yard. Elida was impressed: a swimming pool symbolized status. And in the new house, she had her own wing and bathroom. Less than ten years separated the gleaming shower and bath, with the towels and cosmetics that were hers alone, and the shared bathroom in Mame and Tate's building in Vilna with the big tub in the kitchen.

The pool and family parties brought Elida closer to the extended family. Everyone met on Sundays at their new home, which was also closer to where Lazar's brother lived. The teenage girls would lock themselves in Elida's room, try on dresses, put on makeup, and examine their made-up faces in the big mirror. In their conversations, names of boys their age would come up, and there would be giggles of embarrassment.

Members of the opposite sex began to occupy Elida's thoughts. The books she read were her guides to the vague feelings she felt toward the boys she met when spending time with her cousins. One time, she found herself squeezed into the back seat between two boys. Elida took a liking to one of the boys, Stephen. They all went to the local McDonald's and then to a drive-in. No one paid attention to the movie that flickered on the big screen. Elida was sweating, and her painted red lips shrank into a narrow slit as the boys jostled against her. A boy dressed in a floral Hawaiian shirt, with shiny gel in his hair, poked Elida and said, "Aren't you having fun? Stop being so serious!" Elida glanced at Stephen to see if he was listening, but Stephen was busy gnawing on a hamburger. Next time, I won't be tempted to join them, she told herself.

Toibeh was waiting for her in the kitchen when she returned home. "How was it?" she asked enthusiastically.

"A bunch of brats," Elida replied, hurrying to her room. What luck, she comforted herself, that next year she would already be in college and meet boys who are more serious.

Elida graduated from high school summa cum laude.

At the graduation ceremony, she wore a white gown and white cap, and the teachers and nuns shook her hand in admiration. She was the youngest of the graduates and the most talented. The audience gave her a big round of applause when she was called to the stage to receive her diploma.

NEARLY THREE YEARS AFTER ELIDA ARRIVED AT THE home of Lazar and Toibeh, they decided to expand the family and adopt another girl—this time, a newborn baby.

One Sunday morning, Toibeh and Lazar asked to speak with her. In a solemn voice, Lazar informed her, "Your mother and I have decided to bring you a little sister. We want our family to grow."

Elida stared at them. "What, really? Do you mean that?"

"Absolutely. What do you think?" asked Lazar.

Toibeh was silent, knowing that Elida already knew about their intention to adopt a baby. Elida had gotten wind of their plans from the whispers, the phone calls, the meetings. She had noticed her parents' excitement in recent weeks. Toibeh had asked her a while ago whether she would like to have a brother or sister. Elida wanted that very much. She knew that her arrival had made them feel like family, despite the difficulties and quarrels. She knew how much they wanted children, and now they wouldn't have an "empty nest" when she left home for college. A newborn baby would be her sibling from birth. She had never had anything that was hers from the beginning.

"I think it's a great idea," Elida told them. "Now when I'm at college, it's great that you'll have another boy or girl—and that I'll have a brother or sister."

From the fragments of the conversations, Elida understood that the biological parents were giving away a newborn baby, a Jewish baby. Did that make sense? Her real parents had given her away, too, but they had no choice. There was a war. And here a mother and a father, not during a war, were giving away a newborn baby. What would happen to her? Dickens's books came to mind. David Copperfield was adopted as an orphan, but here the parents were alive. When the baby grew up, she would understand that she was given away. How could Elida help her? She'd understand her better than anyone; only she would know what the girl was going through.

The family left for Dallas in the morning. Accompanied by a lawyer, they entered the hospital, where a nurse in a white uniform handed the baby over to Toibeh. Toibeh and Lazar cried, but Elida's eyes remained dry. Her only concern was that Toibeh would drop the baby. She hesitated to approach and ask to hold the baby. For a moment, she felt left out, but then Lazar called to her, "Come see the baby. Do you want to hold her?"

She approached. Out of the white blanket a tiny head peeked, covered in black curls. A small fist tried to find its way into a small mouth, and the baby's eyes opened and closed intermittently. Elida smiled at her, reached her finger to the baby's fist, and then backed away.

Accompanied by a specially hired private nurse, the family went home to Laredo. On the way back, Elida remarked, "She doesn't have a name yet!"

Toibeh exchanged glances with Lazar. "We were just thinking of possible names," Toibeh told her. "We thought of naming her after my mother, Mira, but would like it to be a Hebrew name as well, so we thought of Amira."

Elida pursed her lips. "Amira? That's not an American name. Maybe it would be appropriate in Israel, but she's an American and the name should be appropriate here!" she said firmly.

"My grandmother was named Dvora, perhaps Deborah?" Toibeh suggested hesitantly.

Elida's face lit up. "Sure, Deborah is Debbie, it's a beautiful name. It sounds really American!"

Lazar, who had not yet intervened in the conversation, turned to Toibeh and asked, "So, what do you say? It's a name that fits and that Elida loves."

"Yes, Debbie, I agree. We'll call her Debbie."

The first few weeks were not easy. The new baby cried a lot, and Toibeh was helpless. Elida was upset.

"The baby is sick," she decided. "Something must be done."

"The doctor saw her just yesterday," Toibeh replied indecisively.

At night, all the members of the household hovered around the baby's crib, but she did not stop crying. Feeding her and rocking her in their hands did not help. Debbie would fall silent for a few minutes and then begin wailing again.

"I'm going to call the doctor!" Elida announced.

"You can't," Toibeh argued with her. "You can't call the doctor in the middle of the night."

"And what if something happens to her?" Elida insisted. She then marched decisively to the telephone and called the doctor. A drowsy voice answered the phone, "Who's speaking?"

"Doctor, I'm speaking from the Goldberg residence. I'm their daughter. You must come, our baby is going to die!"

"What?" the doctor exclaimed. "Let me talk to Mom or Dad."

"That's not possible, they're with the baby. You must come! What if she dies?"

A half an hour later, the doctor arrived. He quickly entered and saw the baby whimpering in Toibeh's arms. "Oh, Doctor, I'm sorry," Toibeh apologized. "My daughter insisted that you come."

The doctor took the baby and examined her from head to toe. The touch of his hands calmed her down. He asked for a bottle of freshly boiled and sweetened water, and Toibeh hurried to prepare it. Debbie sucked the liquid eagerly.

"The baby is fine, she's perfectly healthy," he said confidently. Then he reassured Elida, "Young lady, your sister is not going to die."

"So why is she crying like that?"

"That's how babies cry. That's how they tell us that something is bothering them."

The baby with the black eyes and frizzy hair lit up the world of the Goldberg family.

Elida was a partner in the joy and change that Debbie brought to their home. She loved Debbie and pampered her, but Debbie arrived when Elida was already spreading her wings, preparing to leave Laredo for the first stop in her independent adult life—at the University of Texas at Austin.

6

Elida in the Academic World

On the eve of her departure for the University of Texas, the extended family gathered for dinner at their favorite restaurant. The owner of the restaurant hurried to serve them, showering compliments and culinary suggestions. The Goldbergs were among his most loyal customers. "What do you say about our student?" Lazar asked proudly. "She'll be the youngest of the female students because she skipped a grade!"

Elida straightened up and smiled, watching the many family members gathered in her honor. The last few nights she had trouble sleeping. The suitcases in her room reminded her of the departure from Vilna with Mame and Tate. How different the content of the luggage was now, how different the feeling, she thought. In the past, each transition had been arranged by other people. This was the first time that she was choosing her own path. She had been compelled to adapt to different worlds, to a new family, to a different culture, to a new language. Now she was going to start an independent life.

Thanks to her strong academic record and high SAT scores, Elida was admitted to several prestigious universities, but she and her parents chose UT Austin because it was also located a reasonable distance from their home.

When they returned from the restaurant, Lazar had a serious talk with her. "*Mein kind,*" he said, "you're embarking on a new path and I'm very proud of you. I'm sure you'll be an outstanding student there too. But university is not only about studies; it's also about people. It's learning how to manage on your own. We'll support you, but you also have the responsibility to take care of yourself. And most importantly, don't forget that you're Jewish. Don't date guys who are not our kind or, God forbid, fall in love with one. It's very important to me that you remember who you are."

Elida studied his face. Every fold and crease in it expressed kindness and tenderness. She didn't want to hurt him, but the subject of her Jewishness always aroused her anger. The crisis of her desire to convert to Christianity still stood between them.

"I am what I am. I want to study and advance, and that's why I'm going to the university. Nothing else interests me now," she said.

They switched to talking about the bank account they'd open for her in Austin, and Lazar repeated the list of acquaintances who could assist her. As he spoke, she suddenly noticed that all their conversations were in Yiddish. Maybe if we speak English with each other, things will change a bit, she thought. But in the end, they continued to speak in Yiddish.

For weeks, she was busy inquiring about the university and its curriculum. She asked to hear more and more from her cousins, some of whom had studied there. She was debating what to study. She remembered that she'd once wanted to be a doctor like her biological father, but she was no longer sure about going to medical school. She preferred literature and the arts. Nevertheless, she decided to major in the natural sciences, which was considered a prestigious field at the university.

The campus was full of young men and women walking from building to building in jubilant groups, in pairs, or on their own. I'm one of them, she reminded herself over and over again. The air was hot and humid. The buildings were large and impressive, arranged in columns and separated by lawns and straight sidewalks. In front of the main building, the famous campus tower, was a huge plaza, bordered by straight rows of manicured shrubs. She examined the map in her hands. Where should she go?

A broad-shouldered guy with a cropped haircut approached her with a smile. "Can I help you? You're a new student, right?"

Elida smiled the smile she reserved for the opposite sex. "Yes," she replied. "I'm looking for the way to the dorms."

"I'll accompany you, okay?" His name was Tom, and he was a second-year law student. He asked her where she was from and what she was studying.

"I enrolled in the natural sciences and I'm from Laredo, Texas," she replied.

"Really? You don't sound like you're from South Texas."

He told her that his family was from Dallas and that he chose to study here because his father had also graduated from this university.

They walked slowly side by side. He offered various suggestions about places to go on campus and about university life, and she kept smiling. "Will you come with me and my friends to a bar on Friday night?" he asked. She accepted his invitation.

Elida's dorm room was simple and furnished like the others. It had a bed, a closet, and a desk. At local stores, she purchased a small armchair and a colorful bedspread and pillows. Her roommate was Emily, who came from a well-established family in Waco, Texas. Emily was tall and thin, with black hair scattered over her shoulders, and she spoke in a distinctly Texan accent. Like Elida, she was studying the natural sciences.

Sharing a room was strange to Elida, who set clear boundaries for Emily regarding their belongings and asked her to be quiet and allow her to study without any background music. Elida spoke only briefly and vaguely about her past. At all the social gatherings, she hardly mentioned that she had been born in Lithuania and certainly never mentioned the adoption. Elida just said she was from Laredo. She kept her distance from the Jewish students who often crowded the Hillel clubroom on campus. If any of them had asked her out on a date or invited her to a Jewish social gathering, she would have made excuses and declined.

When she first arrived on campus, Elida believed that the social structure of the student body was homogeneous. To her, they all seemed to be bright and talented students from good homes. But over time, she learned to recognize their diversity. Some students came from conservative Texan towns and others from states outside of Texas. There were elegant girls who led bohemian lives and boys who spent more time on the lawns than in the classrooms, ogling and pestering the coeds. Some of her peers took their studies seriously and spent most of the days in libraries and intellectual pursuits. Elida learned to navigate among the groups and choose the ones that made her feel comfortable. She immediately proved herself an outstanding student, became a member of the prestigious Book Club and was also invited to parties.

Dressing for her first date with Tom, she emptied her entire closet. Emily sat on the bed opposite her, offered her opinion, and hinted to Elida that she would like to join her. Elida chose to ignore the hint. This evening was hers. If she succeeded in winning the hearts of Tom and his friends, it would be a promising start. She opted for new jeans and a white button-down shirt, then swept up her hair, applied a little makeup, and hurried to meet Tom. On the way, she ran into the person in charge of her dormitory, who reminded Elida that she had to return before the doors locked at eleven.

Tom was waiting for her. He surveyed the girl who smiled at him with her brown, almond-shaped eyes. "Oh, nice," he complimented her, and they went out to a bar near the campus.

Dozens of young people with glasses in their hands crowded around the wooden tables in the bar. Tom grabbed her hand and led her to a table of jubilant guys in plaid shirts and shy, giggling girls. Just like a scene in an American movie, Elida thought.

Tom introduced everyone and each greeted Elida in a different way: a wink, an air kiss, or some other gesture. She agreed to a glass of beer though she had never tried its bitter taste. She didn't want to reveal her young age to the rest of those present.

"I'm new here too," one of the girls whispered to her. Elida nodded and made sure she kept smiling.

Elida's friendship with Tom lasted only a few weeks. She did not like his crude jokes, especially when it came to girls. She also realized that his kindness toward her on the first day at the university was also directed at several other girls, who understood what he was after better than she did. Still, she kept meeting with Tom and his friends because one of them caught her attention: Johnny Treadwell. He was tall, with smiling brown eyes and a modest smile. He looked like a movie star, muscular but gentle, the perfect American icon. What's more, Johnny was a star player on the football team, which placed him at the center of campus life.

One afternoon, Elida was with Tom, Johnny, and other friends at a picnic by a river. The boys began to push each other toward the water and the girls cheered them on. Suddenly, Johnny turned toward Elida, swooped her up in his arms, and threw her into the water, to the delight of all present. He then rushed to get her a towel, wrapped her up, and apologized for his action. Instead of getting angry, she curled up in his arms. From that moment on, they were a couple.

As the girlfriend of a football star, Elida soon became one of the most well-known and popular students on campus. Every public appearance of the couple was documented. One picture in the campus newspaper showed Johnny and Elida standing shoulder to shoulder in a Beetle convertible. In another picture, Elida, her hair dyed blond, can be seen standing next to Johnny, smiling happily. "The campus couple," the newspaper declared in the gossip column. Elida also became a regular spectator at Johnny's football games, roaring the slogans and wearing the team colors. Her academic excellence was unquestioned, but her prominent social status on campus surprised everyone.

Elida loved Johnny and he was good to her. On benches in hidden corners, they hugged and kissed, and she was filled with a sense of tenderness. When had she ever felt this way? Mostly in her imagination, when she read in the library. When she read *Anna Karenina,* she felt a longing for love and a mysterious desire pulsed inside her. Now the surging waves within her made her forget every fragment of sadness. She was amazed at the feeling she had in her lower abdomen when they were together.

He complimented her beauty, admired her intelligence, and envied her academic achievements. One time, when she was in his arms, she whispered, "I want to be with you alone, without all the fans and friends and the coach and the team."

"There will be such days," he promised.

"When? Here on campus, you belong to everyone. I feel that I have to share you with everyone."

"You fell in love with a football player, baby." He smiled at her. "But I assure you that next vacation it'll be just you and me."

When Johnny asked her about her past, she answered briefly, "What is there to tell you? I'm from Laredo, a town that has nothing to offer. My parents are wealthy, and they sent me to a private school. And because I excelled at school, I'm a year younger than other first-year students here."

Johnny did not delve into it too much, and she thanked him for that.

He told her about his parents and sister in the Austin suburbs and about his days in high school. His father came to campus to watch all his son's games. He would sit next to Elida in the stands and try to elicit conversation, especially about her background. But, as usual, she responded with only partial information: she was from Laredo and had graduated from Ursuline Academy. Her last name was Goldberg, and her father was a businessman. "Yes, we are Jews," she replied casually, as if to say, "It's an unimportant detail in my life."

When the football team was about to travel to the annual game in Houston, Johnny asked her to come along. But she declined the invitation. "You're my mascot," he begged. "When you sit in the bleachers and I see you, I'm more successful. We can also be together in the evenings. A lot of the girls want to go, why won't you?"

"I can't miss school, you know me. It's very important to me. We have an exam and it's not the right time for me to travel to Houston."

"If we win—and everyone says we definitely have a chance to win—you'll be sorry you weren't with me."

"I'm sure you'll win, and I'll keep my fingers crossed. But I can't come, not this time."

Johnny and Elida, each in their own way, knew that their relationship would not last too long. She enjoyed his closeness and loved the popularity she gained. He marveled at her intelligence but knew their romance was temporary when she expressed astonishment at a book he had never read, when she got angry at his unwillingness to go with her to political debates, and when she rolled her big eyes to express her impatience at hearing endless descriptions of football games, tensions with the coach, and competition between players.

Despite the social temptations, Elida did not give up what she had always loved: studying. "I've always excelled in my studies and don't want to miss the opportunity to excel at university as well," she boasted to her roommate. She loved sitting in the front row in the classroom, listening to her teacher's every word, and was among the first to raise her hand to ask challenging questions. Elida loved the lecturer's surprised look when he heard her say something insightful, and she didn't mind the admiring or jealous glances of her classmates. In laboratory classes, she helped the labs prepare the test tubes and materials for the various experiments. When she told Lazar on one of her vacations about how she enjoyed her lab experiments, he told her quietly, "Just like your mother, who was a lab assistant."

She successfully integrated into science studies, but her first love continued to be books. They had always been her closest and most intimate friends. Her strongest memories of Vilna, which now seemed to belong to another life, were of the books she read and the library in the stone building: the shelves laden with books, the heavy smell of moldy paper, and the literature lessons that introduced her to Russian literature's great writers. She zealously kept these memories to herself. Although Virginia had opened the door to American and English literature, her heart retained its admiration for the Russian language and its literature. Neither Johnny nor any of the people here in America could bond with her life story. In America in the early 1960s, when the Cold War was in full swing, a Russian-speaking student born in the Soviet Union might encounter a wave of suspicion and misunderstanding, and she desperately wanted to be regarded as an American.

Elida found more friends among the members of the book group. Johnny begrudgingly joked that his principal competitor was whatever book Elida was reading. Emily, too, complained that Elida's reading light kept her up at night.

One of Elida's favorite books at the time was J. D. Salinger's *Franny and Zooey,* which was published in 1961 and soon became one of the most talked-about books in intellectual circles. Elida read it in two days, and when she finished, she read it again. The book shook her. She totally identified with Franny; Franny's passion for books was so understandable to her. She imagined herself in the living room in Franny's home, browsing the rows of books—just as she had done in the Kazens' home.

"Books are reflections of ourselves," she told the Book Club. The discussion leader argued that Salinger's book was a social critique of the "ivory tower" of universities and the inflated egos of intellectuals.

"That's not the point," Elida countered. "Salinger emphasizes the gap between the conduct of people in society and their conduct in their inner world. To penetrate Franny's soul, we must penetrate the books she reads."

There was silence in the room. "Is that how you feel?" the leader asked hesitantly.

"I'm not the issue here. The idea is that human beings live a dual existence—the way they conduct themselves outside and what goes on inside their hearts."

After the meeting ended, Jeffrey, one of the few male students in the club, asked Elida if she'd like to go to a coffee shop with him and continue discussing the book. Elida looked at him in surprise and said, "I have a boyfriend—Johnny, the captain of the football team."

"Oh," Jeffrey hissed at her, adjusting his glasses, "that's what you meant when you talked about the inner world and the outer world. And maybe even the ego." He hurried away.

"Idiot," she muttered.

DURING HER MONTHLY HOME VISITS IN LAREDO, ELIDA grew closer to her family, especially her little sister, Debbie. "I missed you so much, just because of you, little monkey, I drove five hours," Elida would say. But she dodged her parents' prying questions.

"Yes, I'm satisfied, the studies are interesting, I pass the exams, I manage with the money, yes, I would love to receive an additional amount, and no, there's nothing special to tell," she would respond to Lazar's inquiries.

In the mornings, after Lazar left the house for business, Toibeh would try to ask other questions. One day she asked her, "What about this Johnny? Is he nice to you? We heard there was a big party, and you were photographed with him for the university newspaper. Maybe you can show me the picture? What did you wear?" Then she continued hesitantly, "You know, you're still young and many more things will change. I can tell you that from my experience. Johnny may be a nice guy, but he's not our kind. He's your first boyfriend, but there will be others."

"I know what I'm doing," Elida replied. "You treat me like a little girl, but I'm already out of the house. I'm a mature student and it's ridiculous to tell me, with everything I've been through, that I have no experience."

"At your age," Toibeh replied to her, "I had survived a war with a number on my arm, alone in the world!"

When the conversation reached this point, Elida left Toibeh and went into her room.

AT THE END OF ELIDA'S FIRST YEAR AT UT AUSTIN, LAZAR bought her plane tickets to Europe and Israel. "We'll travel to Israel, and on the way back, we'll go via Paris and visit my cousin, Nahum Dinner."

Elida took the tickets and flipped them back and forth. A visit to Europe fascinated her. She had heard a lot about Paris—but with Lazar? Again, she would have to open doors to the past; the visit to Israel worried her.

Elida asked, "Will Toibeh and Debbie come too?"

Lazar replied defensively, "We cannot both leave the business all summer, and Debbie is still too young. We'll go just the two of us. You know that for me it's important to go to Israel. I haven't visited there for over a year. Aren't you happy that we'll visit Paris? You deserve a little vacation after studying so hard."

"I don't know, I have to think about it," she replied.

"But I've already booked the flights. I thought you'd be happy."

"It's not that simple for me. If I go, I'll have to visit Tate and Mame," Elida explained.

"That's exactly why I thought you'd want to go," Lazar responded. "I know you've been writing to Mame, and I'm sure she'll want to see how you've grown, how beautiful you look. You can tell her how successful you are. She deserves some pleasure."

Elida bowed her head and was silent. Visit Mame? Lazar was right, she really wanted to see her. Mame, more than anyone else, would be able to see how she had changed. But maybe what they really wanted was to keep her away from Johnny, she thought. She'd be gone for two months. On the other hand, it would be a way to test how much she really missed him.

"I still have to mull it over," she said. Later that day, she told Lazar she would go with him to Israel.

A WAVE OF HEAT AND DUST GREETED THEM AT THE AIRport in Israel. Avraham, a relative, was waiting for them at Lod. When he saw them approaching, Elida noticed how astonished he looked. "Is this Elida? Blond? What a beautiful girl!"

The family gathered at the home of Pinchas and Yehudit. Elida looked around and thought: it's the same family portrait, as if time has frozen since the eve of my trip four years ago. There were cries of admiration. "Totally American! What a hairstyle, and the face, more beautiful than in the pictures." Her hair was lifted high on her head, and she wore a floral summer dress that accentuated her narrow waist. The cousins peered at her; as always, she was different. "How I missed you! How much you've changed for the better!" her aunt Leah said. "Come stay with me during the visit. I've prepared everything to make your stay comfortable and pleasant."

Elida smiled politely at her. "No, thanks, I'm with Lazar at the hotel."

"It's more convenient," Lazar explained, rescuing Elida from the unpleasantness. "We're here for two weeks. We'll be able to see everyone and spend time together."

"When will you go to Kiryat Haim to meet the Ruhins?" Leah continued. "Do you want me to come with you?"

"No," Elida replied. "We invited them to the hotel, and they'll come to see us tomorrow."

In the morning, Elida walked around the lobby restlessly and finally informed Lazar that she was going to wait for Mame outside. She could not decide which was preferable—for Mame to come alone or with Tate.

Mame arrived alone. When she saw Elida waiting for her at the hotel entrance, she burst into tears. She grabbed the shoulders of the girl who had been her daughter and examined her from head to toe.

"*Mein kind*, how beautiful you are. And how big you are, my girl! You're no longer a child!"

Elida responded with a thin smile. She looked around,

glad to see that no one was watching. She had imagined her reunion with Mame so many times, and now that it was happening, she felt embarrassed.

"Tate wanted to come, but he's ill and it's hard for him to ride the bus. He sends his greetings, and you'll see him when you come visit us in Kiryat Haim." Elida led Mame inside.

Lazar, who was waiting in the lobby, stood up. Elida took a closer look at the person who had been her mother for nearly ten years. Wrinkles had multiplied on her face. Elida noticed that she had gone to the hair salon, and that she was wearing a dress they had sent her from Laredo. She felt sorry for Mame and was disappointed that Tate had not come. They sat down, and Mame took out some cake from the basket she was carrying. "I baked you the *babke* cake you love," she said.

"No need, no need," Elida said, pushing it away, annoyed by the rustling of papers in the bag.

"There are other things here that you love," Mame said.

"Later. It's not nice to bring food from outside into a hotel," Elida explained.

Mame sweated, laughed, and cried, stroking Elida's hand. Throughout the visit, Mame never let go of Elida's hand or took her eyes off her face.

"You're beautiful," she said.

The atmosphere gradually became more relaxed. Elida told Mame about the university, her car, the room she had at home, and Debbie, her new little sister.

"And do you miss us a little?" Mame asked, trying to cling to a small part of Elida's new life.

"Yes, yes," Elida replied. "You're the only reason that I came to visit Israel. It's only because of you!"

During the two-week visit, Elida met with Mame several times and also traveled to Kiryat Haim. Tate had grown very old and didn't stop coughing. The misery of the apartment and their loneliness saddened her. The handful of dollars that Lazar stuffed into Mame's hand helped.

"I'll probably come next summer too," Elida reassured Mame as she said goodbye.

Five months later, Tate died.

THE FEW DAYS IN PARIS ON THEIR WAY BACK WERE thrilling for Elida. The beauty of Paris, with its wide boulevards, towers, and statues on every street corner, filled her heart. She spent some time touring on her own. At Notre Dame Cathedral, she entered the chapel and felt an unexplained longing for warmth and love. The smell of the candle wax, the small flames flickering on the walls, the quiet hum of the worshippers, all aroused in her an emotion she could not fathom.

The French language also fascinated her. She listened to its sound as it played in the mouths of the people around her. "I want to learn French," she told Lazar and Nahum Dinner, her Parisian uncle, as they sat down for dinner.

Lazar did not understand Elida's enthusiasm, but Nahum encouraged her. "It's a beautiful language. The greatest literature was written in French. Advanced ideas that influenced the world should be read in the original language.

"I have an idea," Nahum continued, smiling his kind smile. "When you graduate from the university in Texas, you can come to Paris, live with us, and learn French. The Sorbonne has special one-semester courses."

"When she graduates, we'll see," Lazar said. "There's still time."

During her trip, Elida thought of Johnny constantly but still wasn't sure she should stay with him. Was it love? She missed the man who touched her so gently; she missed his body, the Johnny who was alone with her in the car or at picnics by the lake.

But did she miss the other Johnny too? The tinges of jealousy she felt when he paid attention to other girls? The Johnny who had no interest in books?

When she returned to Austin, they arranged to meet at a café near the campus. When Elida arrived, she greeted him with an embrace and smiled, but he averted his eyes. She realized it was a farewell meeting. He apologized and told her he had met Carol.

"She's not like you, but something happened between us," he explained. "And I also felt I need a little more freedom. To be successful in sports, I need to be more unrestricted. Both you and I are too young for a serious relationship."

"I knew this was coming," she replied quietly. "For someone whose whole world is football, there is no room for love."

Johnny smiled. He was relieved. He leaned toward Elida and kissed her cheek. "We had beautiful days together. Let's keep them as a beautiful memory."

ELIDA COMPLETED HER BACHELOR'S DEGREE CUM LAUDE ahead of schedule, and it was clear to her that she would pursue a graduate degree and continue on to a PhD. Academic life fascinated her, but she was not sure what to study and where. "In order to be able to progress and really get to know academic life, I need to leave Austin and go to a university outside Texas," she told Jeffrey, her friend from the Book Club. "Should I continue my science studies or fulfill my family's desire and start medical school? Perhaps I should consider studying literature and languages?"

Jeffrey looked at her admiringly. "Not every student has such a privilege to choose, along with the financial support for tuition and housing. I don't know if my parents can afford any more schooling for me."

Elida narrowed her eyes and watched him intently. Jeffrey knew that look. She wasn't really focused on him, he knew.

"What are you thinking about?" he asked.

"Oh, nothing," she replied.

She had been thinking about the fact that Lazar had never raised the issue of tuition costs, and that she had taken his financial support for granted.

In a letter to Virginia Kazen, Elida wrote:

I know I used to think of becoming a doctor, but that doesn't appeal to me anymore. Jewish parents dream that their child will become a doctor but that doesn't suit me. The natural sciences are interesting, and the studies intrigue me, but from you, Virginia, I learned to love literature. I know that I'm talented in languages and love Russian, French, and English literature. But what could I do with these studies as a profession? Become a teacher? A writer? Maybe I'll study translation and work as a translator.

The answer came from an unexpected direction. For over a year, Elida had served as a research assistant for one of the lecturers in the Chemistry Department. He admired her skill and diligence. At the end of the semester, he summoned her for a conversation. Elida walked to his office thinking that he probably wanted to discuss the results of the latest experiment. She came prepared with the data.

The professor smiled at her and invited her to sit down. "I didn't invite you this time to discuss our research. I received an offer to join the faculty at the University of California in Los Angeles, UCLA, and I'd like to propose that you consider continuing your chemistry studies at UCLA. I can give you a letter of recommendation and I'm sure you'll have no problem getting accepted there."

Elida's eyes opened wide, and her smile broadened slightly. "I appreciate your vote of confidence in me," she said.

"I don't expect an immediate answer," he reassured her. "I suppose you'll need to consult with your family. As for the tuition, I can look into the scholarship options. And if you decide that this offer does not suit your plans, I'll fully understand."

He rose from his chair, signaling to Elida that their conversation was over. She thanked him and left. In the evening, she called Lazar and told him about the offer.

"Los Angeles? So far? In any case, it's a great honor!" he replied.

IN THE SUMMER OF 1961, ELIDA ACCEPTED NAHUM DINNER'S invitation to come and stay at his home in Paris and study French at the Sorbonne. She arrived equipped with a wardrobe, books, and expectations for a particularly interesting period. Living in Paris! Walking around the tall houses adorned with stone carvings and balconies with beautiful latticework, the museums, speaking French! Connecting with Balzac and his devoted Father Goriot, Rousseau, Victor Hugo. To whom could she confide her dreams? French literature! She wanted so much to read it in French.

In an excited letter, she told Virginia Kazen about her trip. Virginia thought it would be wise to offer a cautionary note to curb Elida's expectations. "There are dreams and there are realities," she wrote. "Reality does not always live up to our dreams."

Nahum and Magda's life in Paris was different from

the lives of Lazar and Toibeh. They had a small workshop where they made teddy bears for children. In the past, Nahum had been a lawyer. He studied law in France, returned to Lithuania, and was a respected lawyer there. He and his wife survived the horrors of war and arrived as refugees in postwar Paris. Nahum did not resume his career as an attorney. He and Magda worked hard for a living. Their son, Alex, a high school student at the time, was their pride and joy. Magda, an elegant woman filled with the wisdom of life, made clear to Elida that she'd be assigned household duties. This was unusual for Elida, and she wasn't pleased.

But outside the house, she fit in well. She studied French at the Sorbonne in a class with other foreign students. She teamed up with Natalie, a Harvard student from a wealthy family in the New York area. Natalie shared Elida's love for French literature and admired her knowledge of languages. They strolled the streets of Paris in awe, wandering through the crowded bookstores and markets. "Everything is so different and majestic," Elida wrote to an acquaintance in Texas.

Elida observed the intellectuals who gathered in the cafés on the Left Bank of the Seine, and on Sundays, when no classes were held, she attended prayer services at the Saint-Sulpice Church. As she listened to the organ playing, she was engulfed in serenity. On one occasion, when Natalie joined her at the church and asked what made her connect so deeply with Christianity, she replied, "I feel like I belong there."

Toward the end of her stay in Paris, Elida returned to Nahum and Magda's home and declared, "I want to convert to Christianity." This was a repeat of the episode in Laredo. She did not anticipate the intensity of Nahum's rage, which rivaled Lazar's reaction from years earlier. "If you do that, you will not stay in my house even one day." He pounded the table. "You cannot change who you are."

Elida turned pale and trembled. Magda noticed her clenched fists and quickly tried to calm the situation. "Nahum, please leave us alone to talk."

Magda asked Elida to sit down and handed her a glass of water. She spoke quietly to her. "Such decisions are not made in one day. I understand that your world is turbulent after everything you've experienced in your life, but you must understand that everyone who loves you cannot allow you to make such a critical mistake."

Elida hissed, "Why is it a mistake? If I'm looking for a way that will be good for me, is that a mistake?"

"You haven't examined the reason why you feel that Christianity would be good for you. Let me tell you, I've been through the seven circles of hell in my life, mostly because I'm a Jew. Many of the catastrophes I experienced were the handiwork of Christians. Today I understand that religion in any form can bring about evil, darkness, competition, and desire to control the human psyche. I became an atheist. Have you ever thought about that? Everyone has a right to their inner beliefs, but they should try not to hurt the people close to them. Lazar and Nahum love you and would do anything to make you happy. Let's calm down. Such steps are not taken in one day. Go to sleep. I'll try to calm Nahum down and tomorrow we'll talk again."

In the days that followed, there were more arguments between Elida and Nahum. Everyone realized that it would be best if she left the Dinners' home, so she spent her last week in Paris at a hotel near the university. No one argued with her about moving out. She wanted to say goodbye to Paris quietly and more comfortably.

Elida returned to Texas with a command of French and a love for Paris. She never spoke of her desire to convert to Christianity again. At the beginning of the academic year, she moved to Los Angeles as planned.

7

A New Life

FOLLOWING HER MOVE TO UCLA, ELIDA WROTE to her confidante Virginia Kazen:

> *My life is a series of transitions. I decided to accept the professor's offer and move to Los Angeles. This is a great opportunity to build my life independently. The West Coast is so different from Texas, which is so conservative and provincial. The atmosphere is more open here, and there are no Texas cowboys. I hope I'm not hurting you by saying this. Everything I acquired at your home is guiding me on the path to being a part of the social and academic world.*

In a letter to Toibeh, she noted the girls' free style of dress compared to the modest dresses and conservative attire of the female students in Austin.

Student life suited Elida. She lived in a dormitory with other students from outside of Los Angeles. But her satisfaction with the vibrant campus atmosphere and the independence she felt did not align with the Department of Science. After a few days in the lab, she rushed over to the Literature and Arts Building and scanned the names of the courses and lecturers. She felt a strong attraction to the literary possibilities offered at UCLA. She missed her studies at the Sorbonne and the syllabus of language and literature studies.

That night, she rehearsed conversations with the professor who had invited her to UCLA. She imagined herself explaining to him: "Life in the lab is not right for me. I love literature. It's time for me to do what I've always longed to do." The actual conversation she had with the professor was simpler than she had planned. He showed generosity and understanding. At the end of the conversation, he gave her his blessing.

Elida's life also changed in other ways. During her first year in Los Angeles, she met the love of her life, Richard Katzman. Dick, as he was called by everyone, was a doctoral student with black hair, smiling blue eyes, and a solid physique. Their glances met in the cafeteria. He was a regular there, usually holding a guitar in his hand. She bumped into him at the counter and he stared at her. His eyes continued to follow her as she walked away. He started playing his guitar and soon everyone was singing Pete Seeger's folk songs. As Dick sang, he looked at Elida and she felt he was singing for her. At the end of the evening, they sat down in the corner of the cafe and talked. Elida was attracted to him immediately.

Dick and Elida soon became a couple. Dick was nearing completion of his doctoral studies in biochemistry. He had started as a law student but decided he did not want to become a lawyer and began studying science. He encouraged Elida to study what she loved: languages and literature. Dick was full of personal intellectual charm. He was a political activist on campus and an avid fan of folk and rock music performances.

When Dick told her about his family and his Jewish background, she was in a turmoil. "I'm Jewish too," she told him with an embarrassed smile.

"I didn't think otherwise, with a last name like Goldberg and with eyes like yours," he said happily. But she found it difficult to interpret her own feelings. She wanted to be cosmopolitan, American, and here she was in love with a Jewish guy who proudly declared his Jewishness. "I am not religious. I'm even an atheist. But belonging to the Jewish people is an essential part of me," he explained.

In the first weeks of their relationship, Elida did not mention Dick to Toibeh and Lazar, but Dick's younger brother, Pete, heard about Elida early on. "I'm in love," Dick told his brother, his blue eyes twinkling. "I think I've found the girl I will marry."

Pete smiled. He was used to his brother's dramatic declarations. "Is this like when you studied law and then decided you didn't like it and started studying biochemistry?" he teased him. Yet something in Dick's eager tone made it clear that this time he was serious.

When Pete and his girlfriend, Melena, met Elida, they immediately noticed that she was different from the women Dick had previously dated. They saw how Dick watched Elida with admiring eyes. He put his hand on her shoulder and eagerly swallowed every word she said. She stunned everyone with her intelligence. When the four of them met, the conversation did not revolve around trivial matters but focused on politics, books, and social problems.

"She's one of a kind," Pete told Melena later. "There will be a wedding here. These two are made for each other."

Dick would pull out his guitar and play at every event, and everyone would gather around him. When he was in a good mood, he was a brilliant and vivacious guy, but he was also prone to extreme moods, and his behavior was often unpredictable. Pete managed to downplay some of Dick's more unpleasant behaviors. They were very close, and Elida immediately recognized Pete's influence on his brother. Even though Dick was two years older, Pete took care of him, treating him the way a parent would—and sometimes even beyond that.

Elida understood that Dick's erratic behavior was caused by a medical condition, and she didn't feel threatened by it. She felt close to him and identified with his inner world. Pete's willingness to help also gave her optimism and hope for a better future. So, when Dick asked for her hand in marriage, she didn't hesitate to agree.

Dick's family accepted Elida with open arms, and she

quickly integrated into the family. Dick's parents were Zionist Jews, born in the United States and well educated. They were very different from Lazar and Toibeh—the Holocaust and immigration were not a constant presence as they were in the Goldberg home in Laredo. With Dick's family, she could say goodbye to her past.

The Friday evening gatherings with the Katzman family were celebrations for her. She loved going there. Blossom, Dick's mother, was a warm, smart, energetic, and exemplary hostess. Lou, her husband, was a cheerful and supportive man. These gatherings were always open to other family members. Conversations revolved around worldly affairs. There was no talk of business but of concerts, trips, and books. The past was not a burden. Everyone spoke in English and the topics of conversation captured Elida's heart, reminding her of the Kazen family.

When Elida finally told Toibeh and Lazar that she had met her love and that they had decided to get married, their joy was boundless. Lazar rushed to Los Angeles, and Elida met him at the airport with Dick. There is a picture of the three of them at the airport that reflects Lazar's great happiness.

IN AUGUST 1963, ABOUT THREE MONTHS BEFORE THE wedding, a lavish engagement party was held in Laredo, and the whole family was invited.

In November 1963, the happy couple was married in a

Jewish wedding ceremony in Los Angeles. For the Katzman family, the joy was twofold: Pete and Melena had married just three weeks earlier.

Dick's extended family and friends came to the wedding. On Elida's side, the family from Texas arrived for the wedding, and Aunt Sarah came from Canada with her husband and children.

Under the wedding canopy, Elida felt Mame was missing. Maybe I should have invited her, she thought. Lazar and Toibeh would have been happy to bring her. But she wasn't sure. Maybe Mame's presence would have just reopened her old wounds, she thought. After the wedding, she sent a letter to Mame and attached photos.

Elida was a beautiful bride, with a long white dress that accentuated her slender figure. Dick was also very handsome with his black forelock and elegant suit. The marriage ceremony was held at the home of Dick's parents, followed by a gala dinner in the garden of the Bel-Air Hotel. It was a cheerful wedding, full of joy and optimism. It marked the beginning of a new phase in her life. Dick called her "Lida" and she became Lida Katzman. She spoke fluent English with no trace of a foreign accent. Everyone who spoke to her affirmed her intelligence and education. No one knew anything about her shocking life story.

In Los Angeles, Elida and Dick lived in an apartment not far from his parents' home and Pete and Melena's apartment. They traveled in intellectual circles. Friends who talked about philosophy, politics, and literature would gather at their home. When family members from Laredo arrived, Elida received them very cordially. Havale, Raoul's daughter, was studying in Los Angeles at the time and was often invited to their house. "They are too intellectual for me," Havale told her sister. "When I'm with them and their friends, I feel inferior and out of place."

Elida was busy studying for a bachelor's degree in Slavic Languages, soon followed by a master's degree in Russian Area Studies, while Dick was working to complete his doctorate. In frequent get-togethers with Pete and Melena, Elida always made sure to tell them about Dick's latest academic achievements, as well as her own. Her professors encouraged her to pursue a doctorate, but she decided to take a break from academic life when she became a mother.

At that time, feminism was on the rise. Elida eagerly read Betty Friedan's *The Feminine Mystique* and encouraged her sister-in-law, Melena, to read the book. "Read it, the book is about the frustration of the American woman who has to stay home and find her identity and meaning while caring for children and a husband." Elida identified with this frustration, but she satisfied her intellectual curiosity by reading books. She read extensively in several languages and participated in literature classes.

Elida also managed to work part-time as a research assistant and translator at UCLA's Russian and East European Studies center. A recommendation letter from the center's director described Elida as "efficient, accurate, and industrious" and lauded her "capacity for independent work that was of great benefit to the university."

In January 1965, their eldest son, John, was born. His birth delighted the young couple and the whole family.

A few weeks after the birth, Elida experienced a crisis that today would be called a bout of postpartum depression. When Elida didn't answer the phone for a whole day, Blossom, her mother-in-law, drove over and found John screaming and her in bed, indifferent. They called Toibeh immediately and arranged for medical care; the crisis eventually passed. It was hardly surprising that Elida, who had had such a traumatic childhood, might experience difficulties as a new mother.

Two years later, in 1967, Elida's second son, Alex, was born and affectionately nicknamed Aggie.

Pete and Melena had also become the parents of two children: a daughter, Leslie, and a son, Joshua. The two couples—the Katzmans, as they were called—with their small children often spent time together. Dick took the guitar with him everywhere and would always pull it out to play and sing American folk songs. Groups of young people would join them, and Elida would look at him with admiring eyes.

When he was in a good mood, Dick had a wonderful ability to gather people around him, talk, sing, and rejoice. There was a piano in their house and Dick and Elida would sit next to each other and play for their guests. They also loved classical music. The turntable played in their house nonstop, and there was always a large pile of records next to it, especially performances of works by Chopin. Elida adored Dick's musical side.

But Dick also had dark moods. One evening, the four of them went to a Pete Seeger show. They roared the words enthusiastically but had to leave after Dick swigged down an entire bottle of gin. At another performance, they were sitting outside on the grass when Dick, inebriated, began to play his guitar and sing loudly. People around him tried to silence him because they wanted to listen to the singer. Elida also tried unsuccessfully to quiet him down and finally shouted to Pete, "Come help me get him!" Again they had to leave the concert after Dick caused this commotion.

On Jewish holidays, they would go to Laredo to celebrate with the family. On one occasion, while traveling to celebrate Passover at Raoul's house, Dick drank more than the traditional four glasses of wine and began to make strange noises and behave wildly. Elida got up, picked up the children, and walked off. There was great embarrassment in the house. By then, the immediate family already knew that Dick was an alcoholic, but his outbursts were upsetting nonetheless.

Married life, the difficulties with Dick, and the burden of raising the children brought Elida closer to Toibeh and Lazar. She came to better appreciate their dedication and support and the difficulties they had faced in raising her. She even started calling them Mommy and Daddy, as they had always hoped.

Despite Dick's recurrent incidents, the loving bond between Elida and Dick was still strong. In one of Melena's letters to her mother-in-law, who was on a trip to Europe, she wrote, "Despite his mental difficulties, Elida and Dick support each other. They have love and understanding for each other. I would define it as a symbiotic relationship."

After completing his doctorate in biochemistry, Dick accepted a postdoctoral fellowship at Massachusetts General Hospital, affiliated with Harvard University. It was a great honor to be appointed a researcher at one of the most important hospitals in the United States.

THE YOUNG FAMILY MOVED TO BROOKLINE, MASSACHUsetts, on the outskirts of Boston and close to Harvard University. For Dick, this was an outstanding opportunity. However, the family feared another crisis and thought the move across the country with two young children in tow would be difficult for Elida. But she surprised everyone. She was proud of the fellowship Dick had received and took charge of the transition.

Boston suited Elida intellectually, but she also felt lonely. As she wrote to her sister-in-law: "Dick, as you know, is immersed in his world. He's subject to his changing moods, is absorbed in his work, and doesn't really care what happens to me or the children. It's tough. The weather keeps us at home most of the time and we miss Los Angeles. I apologize for ruining your mood, but I promised to honestly write what's in my heart and so I'm doing that."

Later, Elida's mood improved. In 1969, Toibeh flew to visit her sister in Lithuania and brought Debbie to stay with Elida for the entire summer vacation. Debbie was just four years older than John and six years older than Aggie, so they were like little brothers to her.

During that visit, Elida instilled a love of art and culture in Debbie. She took her to the Museum of Fine Arts, and they both loved spending time there. Debbie was excited as she stood near the large building and looked at the front staircase. The paintings inside stunned her. She stroked the marble statues. An entire world was revealed to her on that visit.

They also visited the Museum of Nature with John and Aggie. They once went with Dick to the Science Museum, and he was proud to present and explain the experiments.

Elida and Dick raised their children very freely, unlike the way Debbie was accustomed to in Laredo. They set up a pool in the yard and the kids ran around on the sand and got completely dirty in the mud. Instead of scolding them, as Lazar and Toibeh would surely have done, Elida just stood there with Dick and laughed with them.

During the Christmas break, Debbie came to visit again and the whole family went skiing in Vermont. Dick took little Debbie up the ski lift and guided her down the hill. When they reached the bottom, Elida was delightedly waiting for them. Debbie spoke often about that vacation.

Elida became pregnant again, and their third son, Tony, was born in 1970. As with the first birth, Elida went through a postnatal crisis. Toibeh was called to Brookline to help restore her daughter's mental and physical health. The dedicated care Toibeh provided during her stay in

Brookline was instrumental in Elida's convalescence. It was a time that family members in Texas and Los Angeles remember as particularly difficult. As the crisis passed, Elida returned to raising her children and supporting Dick. She became very attached to little Tony and called him "my angel."

By the summer of 1970, the family's life had returned to normal. The guests who came to visit were impressed by their hospitality. Rochale, Elida's cousin from Israel, came to visit and lived with them for three months. "Staying with the young family was wonderful," Rochale later recounted. "I didn't feel any tension. Tony was a cute baby, and they took me on walks to see all the sites in and around Boston. They showed me a good time. Elida and her kids went to visit Los Angeles and took me with them. We lived with Melena for three weeks and it was great."

THEY LIVED IN THE BOSTON AREA FOR ABOUT THREE years before relocating again—this time to the University of Memphis in Tennessee. Dick took a position there at the behest of one of his Harvard professors who was moving to Memphis. Transferring to universities in different parts of the country was an accepted part of the academic lifestyle in the United States—but moving with three young children to a new place was not easy. In a letter to her family before the move, Elida lamented: "I still lack a place I can call home." It was the story of her life.

Leaving the Boston area not only meant uprooting the

family, it also prevented Elida from pursuing a promising academic opportunity at Harvard. In late March 1972, she received the following letter from the Admissions Office:

> *Dear Mrs. Katzman:*
> *It gives me great pleasure to inform you that you have been admitted to the Graduate School of Arts and Sciences for the academic year 1972–1973 to study toward the PhD degree in the subject of Slavic Languages and Literature.*
> *Will you be good enough to let me know at your earliest convenience whether or not you accept our offer of admission?*

Elida reluctantly had to turn down this offer from Harvard because the demands of her husband's career were accorded higher priority.

IN MEMPHIS, AS IN BROOKLINE, ELIDA AND DICK BELONGED to liberal groups that sprouted at the universities. In these groups, intellectuals met and discussed political events. These were years of protests and demonstrations against the Vietnam War and against racial discrimination. Elida and Dick were opinionated and active.

While Elida supported the protest movements, she never took part in the demonstrations. Her activism remained within the bounds of debate. In one of the family discussions about the Vietnam War, she said: "Demonstrations won't help. Anyway, the world is run by politicians seeking to boost their own power and economic interests, not only here in America but everywhere. My whole life is a product of these forces." Elida was eerily prescient about this: her whole life would always be ruled by political forces beyond her control.

Gene, her cousin Martha's husband, was an officer in the U.S. Army. He was a Jew, born in Poland before the war. His family fled to Russia and thus survived, and after the war immigrated to the United States. Gene had a close relationship with Elida because they both spoke Yiddish and Russian and because they shared a common past as Holocaust survivors. Although she didn't like to talk about her past, something surfaced in her when she spoke to Gene in Russian, something that was foreign to other family members. Elida and Gene argued about how to relate to the past. Elida insisted on forgetting, saying that whatever had happened in the past could not be changed. She felt lucky to have arrived in the United States, because here she could realize her liberal worldviews.

Gene was proud to be an American military man. When he returned from Vietnam, he stopped by to visit them in Memphis on his way home to Texas. Dick and Elida received him warmly. In the evening, an argument erupted. Elida and Dick condemned the American intervention in Vietnam and Gene, too, for agreeing to serve in an army that committed injustices in Southeast Asia. He left their home feeling very hurt.

Dick had always opposed capitalism and the American consumer culture. He wrote to Pete and Melena as they moved into a new home:

> *Congratulations on your new home. Capitalism has acquired you. Now you're real Americans. Pete, have you bought a Cadillac yet? If so, it fully complements the vision of your class. Or is it a Rolls-Royce? Here in Memphis, life is also materialistic. I've always tried to fight it; you, too, were once on my side. Look where you are now.*

The move to Memphis did not significantly change Elida and Dick's life. It was another stop on the way. They lived in Memphis for less than two years, and by the second year were busy advancing Dick's plan to go to Israel. He had received an offer from the Weizmann Institute to participate in a research program. It was not only the research aspect that attracted him; the opportunity to work in Israel also appealed to his Zionist sensibilities.

Elida objected at first. She still flinched from any Zionist or Jewish connections. She used to complain, "They don't even have toilet paper there yet."

But when they had to make a decision, Elida again acted in accord with Dick's needs and desires—as she had when she gave up the chance to study at Harvard. She wrote to Pete and Melena:

As for the plan to go to Israel: For Dick and his work, it won't be significantly different. A laboratory is a laboratory. For me and the kids, it's a different story. The needs of one always creates a different motivation in the other. That's all there is to say at this point about the matter. I've decided not to waste energy on anything uncertain. Maybe it's not smart or mature on my part, but at least it brings quiet.

8

With the Family in Israel

THE PLANS STARTED TO MATERIALIZE. DICK was invited to join a research team at the Weizmann Institute in Rehovot, Israel. Elida reluctantly went along with the plans. Dick was enthusiastic, filled with Zionist and professional ideas, while Elida was practical. She dealt with packing, farewells, and promises to the children.

In May 1973, the young family arrived in Israel and moved into an absorption center for new immigrants in Haifa. They chose Haifa as their first stop because of its proximity to Elida's extended family. Her arrival in Israel this time was very different from her immigration with Mame and Tate in 1957. Now she arrived as a young woman with a husband, a mother of three sons ages eight, six, and three, full of expectations to adapt to the country with her family.

Her relatives in Israel made every effort to facilitate their absorption. They hosted them, went on trips with them, and reached out to help them through the tangle of bureaucracy. But acclimatization was not easy, mainly because of Dick's health issues and the need to conceal them from the extended family. Elida revealed her difficulties in letters to her parents, to whom she wrote regularly. She wrote the letters in Yiddish using English letters, addressed them as Mommy and Daddy, and signed her letters with expressions of love for them:

> *I hope you're all healthy and that I'll hear from you soon. With us, everything could've been fine if Dick felt better. He's very nervous and usually his head aches or his stomach hurts or he's unable to sleep. If he took his medicines, it would help him, but he doesn't. One day he takes the pills and two days not and I try to get by so that no one will feel my difficulties.*
>
> *Leah looks at me with pitying eyes and asks, "Tell me, how are you?" "Everything is fine," I reply. And I feel lonely. My life is a strange life. I have to be brave, try not to let the kids notice anything. Now that I know nothing will make a difference, it's easier for me to come to terms with the situation. And the situation is living with a sick person, who is difficult to communicate with, who doesn't know what's happening to him, and especially that*

I'm alone. Now I know that his behavior is caused by the disease and is not under his control. What can I do? The difficulty is the loneliness, but nonetheless, I bear the burden. I hope people don't notice anything. Meanwhile, I say that everything is fine. He doesn't know Hebrew, which is easier because he doesn't say his strange words in their language. I hope that with the help of the medication he'll calm down and be able to work.

The kids are fine. The older ones don't speak Hebrew yet. It's little Tony who already knows a few words. The children treat each other and me well. Their behavior is very touching. What's new with you? Write to us, you must understand that times are not easy, and I'm alone. Letters will help.

In some of the letters she sent later, she was more optimistic. In one letter to her parents, she wrote:

I am much stronger and braver than I expected myself to be. The children help a lot, and the family members who visit us often are good to us and show us warmth. This improves our situation here.

In another letter, she added:

What manages to encourage me are the family members—the Merkel family, my aunt, my cousins

Avigdor and Zipi. They visit us, host us, and give me a sense of family. Yocheved Ruhin is also in touch with us. She is very attached to little Tony, and he lets her hug him and kiss him. I feel mostly great pity for her, no more than that. The condition of the children is not bad. Please write about everything, even trifles. Everything interests us. We all miss you.

Elida maintained a close relationship with Pete and Melena. She always regarded them not only as relatives but also as good friends, secret partners, people she could turn to in times of distress. She wrote to them about the problems with Dick that she was trying to hide from the rest of the family. In a letter from July 1973, she recounted her difficulties:

As you can imagine, not everything is as smooth as Dick writes to you. The truth is that things are very difficult. I had to hospitalize Dick for a few days so that his medications, which he refuses to take, could be balanced. At first, I was hesitant about calling a doctor, but when he started raving, I had no choice. There's a doctors' strike here now, and I went through hell to persuade him to be hospitalized. In the meantime, a preliminary loan has arrived from the Weizmann Institute and terms for negotiating Dick's employment at

> *the institute. I don't know who can help me. As I mentioned, I refrain from sharing the problem with my family members here. I hope Dick's hospitalization is temporary and the doctors will find a way to get him out of his situation.*

A few days later, Dick was released from the hospital, as his health condition had improved, and this lifted Elida's mood as well. Nonetheless, she was the more realistic of the two. She wrote to Pete and Melena:

> *Dick's condition is improving. He's full of enthusiasm about everything around him and that doesn't correspond to my own feelings. If you aren't a Zionist, life in Israel isn't easy. It's difficult to enjoy everyday life if there's no compensation in the essential things. I'm emptied of emotions. I'm not connected to my Judaism; this issue is less important to me. I'm more connected to the Western world. For me, living in the United States or England is more meaningful.*

About four months after Elida and Dick arrived in Israel, the Yom Kippur War broke out. It was a turbulent time for everyone. In a phone call to his Israeli relatives during the early days of the war, Lazar groaned in tears, "How many more wars will my child have to go through?"

Because of the war, Elida and Dick's plans were put on hold. In the meantime, they remained in Haifa. It was actually this difficult wartime period that imbued them with a sense of belonging to Israel. In her letters, Elida emphasized her identification with everything that was happening and her pain. She wrote in one letter:

> *You all know the situation in the country. Times are tough now for our family. All the children have been recruited and we identify with them but unfortunately, we can do nothing. In Haifa, everything is quiet. The children are on the Sukkot vacation. The older kids understand what's going on here. Aggie drew a large sign: "Israel wins the war." The little one knows that when he hears a siren, he must go to the "anti-bomb shelter."*
>
> *The people here are brave, and we thank God that the borders are far from the center. The feeling is strange, yet we feel our place is here. This is a very tense time but what is very difficult especially are the losses, the dead. The country is so small, and you feel that each dead soldier is a family member. It's strange and hard to comprehend. It's the rare ability of Israelis to demonstrate an appearance of normality in the most abnormal situation. We hope for an end to the war. For many reasons, for us it means that we can finally settle down.*

In early December, the family moved into a three-bedroom rental apartment in Rehovot. The building was just a short walk from the Weizmann Institute. The older children acclimated to school in the city, and little Tony went to preschool. Elida began looking for work. After a month of searching, she was hired by the Ministry of Absorption at Lod Airport. Her knowledge of languages gave her an advantage in her new role: receiving new immigrants at their first stop in the country. How the wheel turns, she thought. Sixteen years ago, I was a newcomer and I needed help, and now I'm the helper. Elida was very happy about the opportunity that came her way.

Dick wrote a letter to his brother and sister-in-law about the improvement in Elida's self-confidence when she started working. In one of his letters, he wrote:

> *Elida's job enhances her ego and allows her to break free from the house and the four walls that have closed in on her. She also realizes that the children do not need her twenty-four hours a day. In general, the children are adapting wonderfully, and have become independent (in the Israeli style). They wake up on their own, make the beds, and prepare sandwiches for themselves. When they get back from school, they watch Tony. All this until we get back from work. It is very convenient that we are not dependent on a babysitter.*

The family's relationship with the cousins in Israel deepened, but still, there were problems. Elida wrote to Pete and Melena:

It hurts to write to you again with bad news. Dick was hospitalized again. They're trying to balance his medication and cleanse him of the alcohol he drinks nonstop. In my dealings with the doctors, I don't understand them properly. They talk to me in psychiatric terms, and I get lost both mentally and rationally. Let's put the truth on the table. Dick hasn't been healthy all year long. He has had better times but also worse ones. The fact that he is taking medication and drinking alcohol indiscriminately does not improve the situation. Please understand that I cannot continue in the current situation. The options I face are difficult and unsolvable.

One solution I'm currently considering is to go with the kids to Laredo, where they'll get the love and care they need. But the problem is of course Dick. He cannot be left alone. He must have someone by his side. I don't want to throw the problem at you, but I'd be very grateful if you could advise me what to do. Please don't blame me if I leave. There is no question of guilt here. It's a problem of three unfortunate children who cannot live in the situation of having an alcoholic father and I really cannot leave Dick alone. What will happen to him if I take him back to the U.S.? (Another possibility to consider.) What will happen to his work? Here he manages to work. I'm sorry to bother you but I'm not strong enough to carry it on my own—I'm waiting for your advice.

In June 1974, Lazar visited Israel. Dick was released from the hospital and his condition improved. Dick, and especially Elida, shared with Lazar the dilemma of whether to return to the U.S. or stay in Israel. It was finally decided that the children would fly to California and then to their grandparents in Texas.

The days before the flight were fraught with great tension between Elida and Dick. One evening, Dick and Elida sat down with their two older boys and told them they'd be staying in California for the summer vacation and that Mom would be coming too. In a month or two, maybe Dad would join them.

In another conversation, they told the children that they were about to separate because Elida wanted to return to the U.S. to live near her parents, while Dick was interested in staying in Israel. Dick took Aggie for a separate talk, explaining to him that he could choose whether he wanted to live in the U.S. with Mom or in Israel with Dad because that was the country Jews should live in.

As in previous crises, Elida and Dick managed to mend the rift between them. "If Dad gets a job in the U.S., we'll all go back," she told the children. "If not, we'll all go back to Rehovot."

Dick and Elida said goodbye to Aggie and John, who flew to Los Angeles to be with their uncle and aunt, Pete and Melena. "Be good and well-behaved children," their mother whispered in their ears before they boarded the bus that took them to the plane.

The boys stayed with Pete and Melena for over a month and then went to Laredo to stay with Lazar and Toibeh. During that time, Tony remained with Elida and Dick. Toward the end of the summer vacation, Toibeh came to visit Elida and Dick and then took Tony back to Laredo with her. In a letter to Pete and Melena, Elida wrote:

> *A whole month has passed since the kids left home and I've never felt as lonely and sad. And now my mother, who was staying with us, has taken Tony with her to Laredo. Now that all three are there, I cannot find a place for myself.*
>
> *Dick feels better. He's calm and pleasant, as we know him to be. Meanwhile, another dilemma: I was promoted to the rank of supervisor at my job at the Ministry of Absorption. As a result, the nature of the work has changed. I will no longer work night shifts at the airport but my workday is in the morning and afternoon so I can be with the kids. Dick also has a lot of work to do at the Institute after a month away from it. My new job is challenging and requires much more responsibility. These developments have raised the question again: Should we return or stay here? Meanwhile, Dick is planning a vacation trip to Italy. A conference of biochemists is scheduled for early September. He really wants me to join him. The purpose of our trip to the conference is, in part, to meet his boss from*

Boston, who will be there as well. The developments cause us a lot of indecision, and neither of us is the decisive type.

Two weeks before leaving, Elida and Dick were still debating whether or not to return to Israel after reuniting with their children in the U.S. As noted in her letter to Pete and Melena, one of the reasons for the trip to Italy was to meet with Dick's boss in order to explore the possibility of returning to Boston. Elida wrote in a letter to her parents:

> *We don't yet rule out returning to Israel. Here, jobs are guaranteed for both of us. In the meantime, we plan to travel to Italy on Sept. 8 and stay there 10–12 days until the 20th. Later, I'll have more precise details. I don't want to leave the children as a burden to you for so long. I'll come to you either in late September or early October. Kiss the children for me. My darlings, I appreciate everything you're doing for the children.*

IT STARTED AS A ROUTINE SEPTEMBER SUNDAY. THE GOLDberg brothers and their children were planning to meet at Lazar and Toibeh's home for a pool party. Toibeh stood in the kitchen with Maria and prepared food for the guests. The grandchildren, John and Aggie, were all over the house, quarreling and giggling alternately. They insisted on going out into the yard to see the pool filling up with water.

Suddenly the children heard Lazar cry: "Oi vey, oi vey! It can't be! *Dos ken nisht sein!*"

Toibeh hurried over to him. "What happened?" She grabbed his hand and tried to stop him from pacing back and forth. Lazar pointed at the radio.

"The plane fell," he murmured. "The plane fell!"

"What, what?" Toibeh shouted at him and turned the volume up.

The radio reported that a TWA plane had taken off from Israel, landed in Athens for a stopover, and then exploded immediately upon takeoff. Rescuers were trying to locate the remains of the plane off the coast of Greece. There were about one hundred and twenty passengers and crew on board.

"Dick and Elida were on this plane," Lazar moaned. "Oh, Jonah! What have we done wrong in our lives?" he cried, evoking the name of Elida's father. "Oh, Jonah!"

Toibeh watched him and gazed at the radio, unable to utter a word. The children had heard Grandpa's screams and rushed in to see what had happened. Toibeh grabbed their hands and dragged them away.

"Be quiet!" she shouted at them in Yiddish and then asked them in English to go into Debbie's room immediately. She then ordered Debbie to get out of bed and watch the children.

Toibeh hurried back to Lazar, who was standing with his hand on the telephone dial. "How do you know they were on that plane?" she shouted at him. "They flew El Al, not TWA," she said hopefully.

"No, I talked to them yesterday. Elida told me she changed the tickets because the TWA flight would continue on to the U.S." He kept shaking from side to side, choking on tears.

"And you're sure they were flying today?" Toibeh asked, trying every possible chance.

But Lazar knew.

He started thinking about whom to call. The first to come to mind were the Katzmans in Los Angeles. But Toibeh grabbed the phone from him. "No! No!" she cried, and slammed the phone down. "First we need TWA to check whether they were among the passengers."

The front doorbell rang. Maria opened and told Raoul and Angelina in Spanish that something terrible had happened. They hurried into the room and cried out in anguish when they heard what it was all about.

"Maybe they weren't on the plane—they changed their plans so many times," Toibeh said, trying to maintain a glimmer of hope.

But that last glimmer of hope was extinguished when the phone rang. Lazar, shaking all over, picked up the phone. He heard a hesitant female voice on the line. The woman introduced herself as a TWA representative. He listened in silence.

Angelina began to make arrangements. First, she had to get the kids out of the house. She called a mutual friend and asked her to come and take Elida's three children for outdoor activities.

Debbie, who was beginning to grasp what was going on,

could not be persuaded to leave the house. She had been eagerly awaiting Elida's visit. She had worked hard to lose weight and even went to the hairdresser to get her hair done the way Elida loved it. Debbie's feeling of grief and loss combined with her disappointment that her big sister would never get to see her new appearance.

The nephews who started arriving for the pool party were also sent home. Phone calls streamed in from the family in Israel. In Israel, they knew that Elida and Dick had been on that ill-fated plane.

Then came another phone call from the Katzman family. Pete was on the line. The airline had also called Dick's family, confirming that Dick and Elida were on the plane that crashed into the sea off the coast of Greece, leaving behind only a trail of foam on the surface. Pete said he'd catch the next flight to Texas in order to be with Dick and Elida's children.

An investigation into the disaster revealed that an explosive device had been planted in the plane by a terrorist.

Epilogue

FOR THIRTY-ONE YEARS, ELIDA LIVED AMONG us. She left three orphans, who were adopted by Pete and Melena. The three children live in the United States. John is married to Patricia, and they have two children. Alex and his wife, Shirley, also have two children. Tony has a son. One of the reasons I set out to write this book was so that Elida's children and grandchildren would learn her full story. I am grateful to them for their help and understanding.

Writing Elida's story took years of rummaging through books, perusing press clippings, conducting interviews with family members who lived with Elida, traveling to the stations of her life, flipping through albums, and discovering documents that sometimes surprised me. All of these helped me embroider her character and reveal the turning points in her life.

As Elida's story came to light, my feelings of closeness and love for her grew ever stronger. During the writing process, I experienced much emotional turmoil, some of which I share below.

How do you tell a story about a father who handed over his newborn daughter? About a mother who washed her in tears? What strength these parents had to summon in order to tear themselves away from their daughter and place her in the care of strangers, even if it was the only path of hope for her?

While I was writing the story of the baby's delivery, two of my children enriched me with two new grandchildren. I held them in my arms on my visit to the hospital, cradled them close to my heart, and anxiety flooded me. How do you hand over your child to strangers? I will never have an answer for that.

During my visits and meetings in the United States, I was given access to Toibeh and Lazar's secret cabinet. I received a treasure trove of letters and photos from Elida's life, including letters she wrote while she was with her family in Israel. The willingness of those closest to her to entrust all this to me touched my heart. Alex, Elida's son, was especially supportive, and he soon became a full partner in discovering the hidden events in his parents' lives.

We had a thrilling experience during a visit to Lithuania in July 2015. My husband and I traveled with Alex and his family to meet Stanislava's daughter, Audra, who had been a sister to Elida on the farm in their childhood.

It turned out that for years she had been trying to track down Rita-Elida. Great excitement gripped everyone present when she handed Alex an invaluable gift: a tin box with letters and pictures of Jonah and Tzila, Elida's parents and Alex's grandparents. The box and its contents were the most intimate message from the past for all of us.

There were also exciting encounters with many family members who encouraged me to tell Elida's story and shared their memories with me. They all told me that every year, on Holocaust Remembrance Day, they tell Elida's story to their children and grandchildren.

During my journey of writing the book, I was troubled by the thought of what Elida would say about the liberty I had taken in writing the story of her life and invading her inner world. I hoped, and I still hope, that wherever her spirit is, she accompanies me and understands the passion that burned in me to tell our children and future generations what happened to her and to other children who survived the inferno, children who paid a heavy price for the horror they experienced. I apologize to Elida and Dick for daring to tell their story.

Lazar's gravestone in the Haifa cemetery memorializes the name of his six-year-old son, Moshe, who was murdered in the ghetto, and of Elida, in whose memory they wrote: "She was born in the Holocaust and perished in a terrorist act."

As Toibeh would say whenever she spoke of Elida: "Born in fire and died in fire."

Afterword

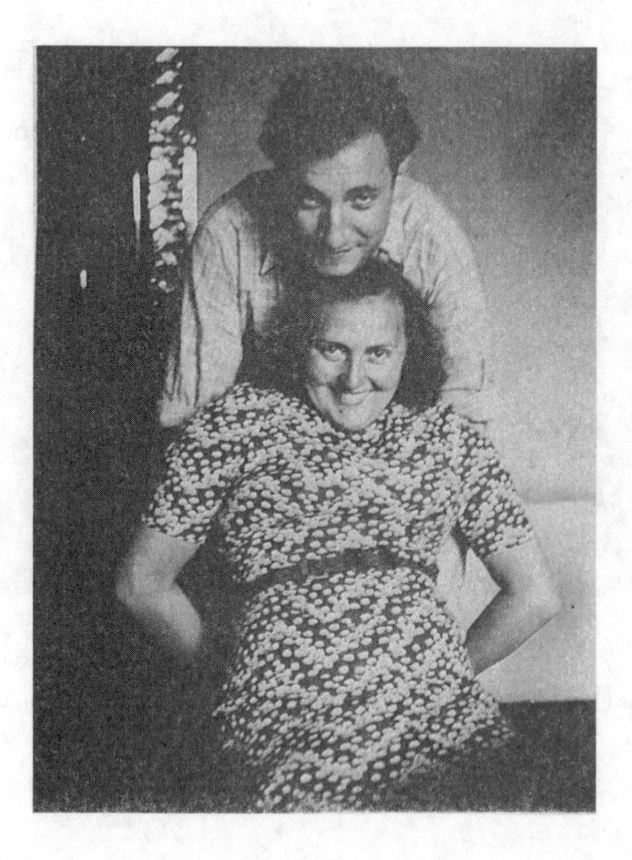

Elida's parents, Tzila and Dr. Jonah Friedman,
before the war

Rita (Elida) with Stanislava and Audra on the farm, 1945

Gita (Elida), age 6 or 7, c. 1951. The original picture showed her adoptive parents Yocheved and Joel Ruhin. Elida cut them out.

Elida (far left) with her school friends

Elida (far right) with her family in Haifa

Elida and Lazar Goldberg meet for the first time in Haifa, July 1957

The first Seder with the Goldbergs in Laredo, c. 1962

Lazar, Debbie, Elida, and Toibeh, c. 1963

Elida and Johnny at a football event at UT Austin

Toibeh, Elida, and Lazar at Elida's wedding in 1963

Elida and Dick Katzman in 1965

Elida, Dick, and their sons upon arriving in Israel in 1973

Elida's children (left to right): John, Tony, and Alex

Elida and Dick's grandchildren at Evan's Bar Mitzvah, 2014: (left to right) Cameron (John's son), Evan (Alex's son), Max (Tony's son), Yona (Alex's son), and Lindsey (John's daughter).

Acknowledgments

MANY PEOPLE ACCOMPANIED ME ON THE long journey that gave birth to this book. Elida's story came to life thanks to my family members, whose memories intersected with my own and who added their testimonies and insights. They encouraged me to dare and write. Thus, the character of our family and Elida's life journey will be immortalized, and her story will be a memorial to our family and heritage.

First and foremost, I owe a debt of gratitude to Elida and Dick's children—John, Alex, and Tony—for allowing me to tell the story of their mother's painful life journey.

I owe special thanks to Alex Katzman, who gave me his blessing and allowed me to break through the emotional barrier and start writing. Throughout the years that I researched and wrote, Alex supported me and encouraged me not to give up and to keep going. Thanks to Alex and his wife, Shirley, my husband, Jossi, and I traveled with them on a "roots" expedition in Kovno and Vilna, an exciting journey that uncovered many important details about Elida's childhood.

Many thanks to Debbie Goldberg, Elida's sister. The conversations I had with her were very moving. She showed me the letters and testimonies kept in Toibeh and Lazar's home. She persuaded Toibeh to share her photos and letters with me.

Two years before the book was completed, my aunt Toibeh passed away before she had a chance to read it. I enjoyed many trips and vacations with her in Israel and in the United States. She was usually silent about her wartime experiences yet unveiled many details about her own life and Elida's life that were buried deep within her.

To the late Pete Katzman, Dick's brother and Elida's brother-in-law, and to his wife, Melena, I owe a great big thank-you. Unfortunately, Pete passed away a year before the book was completed. Pete and Melena were the first to provide me with letters, pictures, and stories. They hosted me at their home and opened their hearts to me in hours of conversation. Both were important figures in the lives of Dick and Elida. They adopted the three orphaned boys and gave them a home in their warmhearted way.

Thanks to the "Goldberg tribe" in the United States—Moy, Thelma, Havale, Martha, and Gene—who hosted me on my travels to the United States to gather information for the book. They all encouraged me to tell Elida's story and illuminated important chapters of her life with her family in the U.S. And thanks to the descendants of the Goldberg and Freidman-Spiegel families in Israel.

To the "parents' generation"—two of my aunts, whose

longevity enabled me to interview them for this book. My beloved aunt Yaffa Goldberg-Tabris answered my questions but still made sure to hide more than she told. I understood her. The pain still choked the words inside her. My late aunt Leah Freidman-Spiegel passed away at the age of 106, lucid and willing to share her family story. She gave me letters written to her by Elida's father, in Hebrew, told me about his character, and entrusted me with important pictures from the past. I thank her children, Muki Spiegel and Rachel Spiegel-Karniel, for expanding my knowledge of the family.

To the "children's generation"—I received great encouragement from my generation and our descendants. It was important for everyone to shed light on our family history during the horrific war and the loss of family members who perished in Lithuania. Today, we understand that our parents hid from us the fate of their siblings and parents to protect us from the horror. In our conversations, we expressed the sorrow of not being able to ask and learn more about the past.

To my cousins Moshe Goldberg and his wife, Raya, and Sonia and her husband, Dodik, who told me about Elida's childhood in Vilna and described life in postwar Vilna. They read the final draft and confirmed the descriptions of life in Vilna at that time. Their approval was very important to me.

To my big brother, Avigdor Klein-Sagi, who passed away four years ago, and to his wife, Alina. Avigdor was

Elida's soul mate during her years in Israel. I thank my kindhearted brother and am sad that he did not have a chance to read the book in which he played an important part.

To my brother Micha Klein and his wife, Shuli, who listened patiently to my stories about writing.

I was lucky to have wonderful support from my cousin Nili Shapira, who grew up with me and is like a sister to me. She was a constant source of encouragement, and her support was invaluable. I am also grateful to her husband, Arale, and her children, who read, encouraged, and translated letters and articles.

I cannot express the full gratitude that goes to my nuclear family, who always knew how to be patient and help in their kind and gentle way and understood my need to focus on writing the book. A big and special thank-you goes to my very dear husband, Jossi Jakob; to my beloved children, Yoav, Roni, and Yuval; to my daughters-in-law, Tali and Tehila, and to my son-in-law, Gal; and to my grandchildren. Jossi endlessly contributed his time and attention, spared nothing, and stood by my side in everything he could with vigor and great wisdom.

Many friends, coworkers, and students were always willing to contribute their sound advice and encouragement, each in their own way. Though I won't cite your names here, fearing that I might skip someone, I am grateful to all of you.

Thank you to my friend Yoram Shapira for undertaking

the initial translation of the book from Hebrew to English. His enormous wisdom allowed the book to reach a worldwide readership.

Special thanks to Ira Moskowitz for editing the English version of my book. His professionalism and patience enabled me to complete the mission of translating and editing the text.

Special thanks to Sara Nelson, my editor at HarperCollins, for recognizing the importance and value of the book and for all her efforts to bring Elida's life story to a broad reading audience.

And thank you to everyone who reads this book. By reading Elida's story, you are helping to keep her memory alive in our world.

About the Author

ZIPORA KLEIN JAKOB HOLDS ACADEMIC DEGREES IN LITERature and history. She was a high school history teacher, a pedagogical counselor for university history education, and the manager of the Educator's Promotion Division at the Open University. She also coaches memoirists.